PARIS SPLEEN

CHARLES BAUDELAIRE

PARIS
SPLEEN

1869

TRANSLATED FROM THE FRENCH BY
LOUISE VARÈSE

A NEW DIRECTIONS BOOK

Library of Congress Catalog Card Number: 48-5012

ISBN 978-0-8112-0007-3

English translation made from the French text of *Oeuvres de
Baudelaire*, La Pleiade, 1931.

ACKNOWLEDGMENTS
For permission to reprint the copyrighted translations in the
"correspondence" section of this volume the Publisher is indebted
to the following translators and publishers: Thomas Cole, editor
and publisher of *Imagi* for the translation "Invitation To The
Voyage" by Richard Wilbur and the Harvill Press, Ltd., and
Pantheon Books, Inc., for translations by Roy Campbell from
Poems of Baudelaire, Copyright 1952 by Pantheon Books, Inc.,
and to Frederick Morgan and David Paul whose translations first
appeared in *The Flowers of Evil*, New Directions, 1962.

Manufactured in the United States of America
New Directions books are printed on acid-free paper

First published as New Directions Paperbook 294 in 1970

Published simultaneously in Canada by Penguin Books Canada Limited

New Directions Books are published for James Laughlin
by New Directions Publishing Corporation,
80 Eighth Avenue, New York 10011.

TWENTY-NINTH PRINTING

CONTENTS

	To Arsène Houssaye	ix
I.	The Stranger	1
II.	The Old Woman's Despair	2
III.	Artist's Confiteor	3
IV.	A Wag	4
V.	The Double Room	5
VI.	To Every Man His Chimera	8
VII.	Venus And The Motley Fool	10
VIII.	The Dog And The Scent-Bottle	11
IX.	The Bad Glazier	12
X.	One O'Clock In The Morning	15
XI.	The Wild Woman And The Fashionable Coquette	17
XII.	Crowds	20
XIII.	Widows	22
XIV.	The Old Clown	25
XV.	Cake	28
XVI.	The Clock	30
XVII.	A Hemisphere In Your Hair	31
XVIII.	*L'Invitation Au Voyage*	32
XIX.	The Poor Child's Toy	35
XX.	The Fairies' Gifts	37
XXI.	The Temptations or Eros, Plutus And Fame	40
XXII.	Evening Twilight	44
XXIII.	Solitude	46
XXIV.	Projects	48
XXV.	The Beautiful Dorothea	50

XXVI.	The Eyes of The Poor	52
XXVII.	A Heroic Death	54
XXVIII.	Counterfeit	58
XXIX.	The Generous Gambler	60
XXX.	The Rope	64
XXXI.	Vocations	68
XXXII.	The Thyrsus	72
XXXIII.	Get Drunk	74
XXXIV.	Already!	75
XXXV.	Windows	77
XXXVI.	The Desire To Paint	78
XXXVII.	The Moon's Favors	79
XXXVIII.	Which Is The Real One?	81
XXXIX.	A Thoroughbred	82
XL.	The Mirror	83
XLI.	Sea-Ports	84
XLII.	Portraits of Mistresses	85
XLIII.	The Gallant Marksman	90
XLIV.	The Soup And The Clouds	91
XLV.	The Shooting Gallery And The Cemetery	92
XLVI.	Loss Of A Halo	94
XLVII.	Miss Bistoury	95
XLVIII.	Any Where Out Of The World	99
XLIX.	Beat Up The Poor	101
L.	The Faithful Dog	104
	EPILOGUE	108

PARIS SPLEEN

TO ARSENE HOUSSAYE

My DEAR FRIEND, I send you a little work of which no one can
say, without doing it an injustice, that it has neither head nor
tail, since, on the contrary, everything in it is both head and
tail, alternately and reciprocally. I beg you to consider how
admirably convenient this combination is for all of us, for you,
for me, and for the reader. We can cut wherever we please, I my
dreaming, you your manuscript, the reader his reading; for I
do not keep the reader's restive mind hanging in suspense on
the threads of an interminable and superfluous plot. Take away
one vertebra and the two ends of this tortuous fantasy come
together again without pain. Chop it into numerous pieces and
you will see that each one can get along alone. In the hope that
there is enough life in some of these segments to please and to
amuse you, I take the liberty of dedicating the whole serpent
to you.

I have a little confession to make. It was while running
through, for the twentieth time at least, the pages of the famous
Gaspard de la Nuit of Aloysius Bertrand (has not a book known
to you, to me, and to a few of our friends the right to be called
famous?) that the idea came to me of attempting something in
the same vein, and of applying to the description of our more
abstract modern life the same method he used in depicting the
old days, so strangely picturesque.

Which one of us, in his moments of ambition, has not
dreamed of the miracle of a poetic prose, musical, without
rhythm and without rhyme, supple enough and rugged enough

to adapt itself to the lyrical impulses of the soul, the undulations of reverie, the jibes of conscience?

It was, above all, out of my exploration of huge cities, out of the medley of their innumerable interrelations, that this haunting ideal was born. You yourself, dear friend, have you not tried to translate in a song the *Glazier's* strident cry, and to express in lyric prose all the dismal suggestions this cry sends up through the fog of the street to the highest garrets?

To tell the truth, however, I am afraid that my envy has not been propitious. From the very beginning I perceived that I was not only far from my mysterious and brilliant model, but was, indeed, doing something (if it can be called *something*) singularly different, an accident which any one else would glory in, no doubt, but which can only deeply humiliate a mind convinced that the greatest honor for a poet is to succeed in doing exactly what he set out to do.

Yours most affectionately,

C. B.

THE STRANGER

TELL ME, enigmatical man, whom do you love best, your father, your mother, your sister, or your brother?

I have neither father, nor mother, nor sister, nor brother.

Your friends?

Now you use a word whose meaning I have never known.

Your country?

I do not know in what latitude it lies.

Beauty?

I could indeed love her, Goddess and Immortal.

Gold?

I hate it as you hate God.

Then, what do you love, extraordinary stranger?

I love the clouds...the clouds that pass...up there...up there...the wonderful clouds!

THE OLD WOMAN'S DESPAIR

A WIZENED little old woman felt gladdened and gay at the sight of the pretty baby that every one was making such a fuss over, and that every one wanted to please; such a pretty little creature, as frail as the old woman herself, and toothless and hairless like her.

She went up to him all nods and smiles.

But the infant, terrified, struggled to get away from her caresses, filling the house with his howls.

Then the old woman went back into her eternal solitude and wept alone, saying: "Ah, for us miserable old females the age of pleasing is past. Even innocent babes cannot endure us, and we are scarecrows to little children whom we long to love."

ARTIST'S CONFITEOR

How POIGNANT the late afternoons of autumn! Ah! poignant to the verge of pain, for there are certain delicious sensations which are no less intense for being vague; and there is no sharper point than that of Infinity.

What bliss to plunge the eyes into the immensity of sky and sea! Solitude, silence, incomparable chastity of the blue! a tiny sail shivering on the horizon, imitating by its littleness and loneliness my irremediable existence, monotonous melody of the waves, all these things think through me or I through them (for in the grandeur of reverie the ego is quickly lost!); I say they *think*, but musically and picturesquely, without quibblings, without syllogisms, without deductions.

These thoughts, whether they come from me or spring from things, soon, at all events, grow too intense. Energy in voluptuousness creates uneasiness and actual pain. My nerves are strung to such a pitch that they can no longer give out anything but shrill and painful vibrations.

And now the profound depth of the sky dismays me; its purity irritates me. The insensibility of the sea, the immutability of the whole spectacle revolt me . . . Ah! must one eternally suffer, or else eternally flee beauty? Nature, pitiless sorceress, ever victorious rival, do let me be! Stop tempting my desires and my pride! The study of beauty is a duel in which the artist shrieks with terror before being overcome.

A WAG

PANDEMONIUM of New Year's Eve: chaos of snow and mud churned up by a thousand carriages glittering with toys and bonbons, swarming with cupidity and despair; official frenzy of a big city designed to trouble the mind of the most impervious solitary.

In the midst of this deafening hubbub, a donkey was trotting briskly along, belabored by a low fellow armed with a whip.

Just as the donkey was about to turn a corner, a resplendent gentleman, all groomed, gloved, cruelly cravated and imprisoned in brand new clothes, made a ceremonious bow to the humble beast, saying as he took off his hat: "A very happy and prosperous New Year to you!" Then he turned with a fatuous air toward some vague companions, as though to beg them to make his satisfaction complete by their applause.

The donkey paid no attention to this elegant wag, and continued to trot zealously along where duty called.

As for me, I was suddenly seized by an incomprehensible rage against this bedizened imbecile, for it seemed to me that in him was concentrated all the wit of France.

THE DOUBLE ROOM

A ROOM that is like a dream, a truly *spiritual* room, where the stagnant atmosphere is nebulously tinted pink and blue.

Here the soul takes a bath of indolence, scented with all the aromatic perfumes of desire and regret. There is about it something crepuscular, bluish shot with rose; a voluptuous dream in an eclipse.

Every piece of furniture is of an elongated form, languid and prostrate, and seems to be dreaming; endowed, one would say, with a somnambular existence like minerals and vegetables. The hangings speak a silent language like flowers, skies and setting suns.

No artistic abominations on the walls. Definite, positive art is blasphemy compared to dream and the unanalyzed impression. Here all is bathed in harmony's own adequate and delicious obscurity.

An infinitesimal scent of the most exquisite choosing, mingled with the merest breath of humidity, floats through this atmosphere where hot-house sensations cradle the drowsy spirit.

Muslin in diaphanous masses rains over the window and over the bed, spreads in snowy cataracts. And on this bed lies the Idol, the sovereign queen of my dreams. But why is she here? Who has brought her? What magic power has installed her on this throne of revery and of pleasure? No matter. She is here. I recognize her.

Yes, those are her eyes whose flame pierces the gloaming; those subtle and terrible eyes that I recognize by their dread mockery! They attract, they subjugate, they devour the imprudent gaze. Often I have studied them — black stars compelling curiosity and wonder.

To what good demon am I indebted for this encompassing atmosphere of mystery, silence, perfume and peace? O bliss! What we are wont to call life, even in its happiest moments of expansion, has nothing in common with this supreme life which I am now experiencing, and which I relish minute by minute, second by second.

No! there are no more minutes, there are no more seconds! Time has disappeared; it is Eternity that reigns, an eternity of bliss!

But a knock falls on the door, an awful, a resounding knock, and I feel, as in my dreams of hell, a pitchfork being stuck into my stomach.

Then a Spectre enters. It is a bailiff come to torture me in the name of the law; it is an infamous concubine come with her complaints to add the trivialities of her life to the sorrows of mine; it is a messenger boy from a newspaper editor clamoring for the last installment of a manuscript.

The paradisiac room and the idol, the sovereign of dreams, the *Sylphid,* as the great René used to say, the whole enchantment has vanished at the Spectre's brutal knock.

Horrors! I remember! Yes, I remember! this filthy hole, this abode of eternal boredom is truly mine. Look at the stupid, dusty, dilapidated furniture; the hearth without fire, without embers, disgusting with spittle; the sad windows where rain has traced furrows through the dust; manuscripts covered with erasures or unfinished, the calendar where a pencil has marked all the direst dates!

And that perfume out of another world which in my state of exquisite sensibility was so intoxicating? Alas, another odor has taken its place, of stale tobacco mixed with nauseating mustiness. The rancid smell of desolation.

In this narrow world, but with plenty of room for disgust, there is one object alone that delights me: the vial of opium:

an old and dreadful love; and like all mistresses, alas! prolific in caresses and betrayals.

Oh! yes! Time has reappeared; Time is sovereign ruler now, and with that hideous old man the entire retinue of Memories, Regrets, Spasms, Fears, Agonies, Nightmares, Nerves, and Rages have returned.

I can assure you that the seconds are now strongly accented, and rush out of the clock crying: "I am Life, unbearable and implacable Life!"

There is only one Second in human life whose mission it is to bring good news, *the good news* that causes every one such inexplicable terror.

Yes, Time reigns; he has resumed his brutal tyranny. And he pokes me with his double goad as if I were an ox. "Then hoi, donkey! Sweat, slave! Man, be damned and live!"

TO EVERY MAN HIS CHIMERA

UNDER a vast gray sky, on a vast and dusty plain without paths, without grass, without a nettle or a thistle, I came upon several men bent double as they walked.

Each one carried on his back an enormous Chimera as heavy as a sack of flour, as a sack of coal, as the accoutrement of a Roman foot-soldier.

But the monstrous beast was no inanimate weight; on the contrary, it hugged and bore down heavily on the man with its elastic and powerful muscles; it clutched at the breast of its mount with enormous claws; and its fabulous head overhung the man's forehead like those horrible helmets with which ancient warriors tried to strike terror into their enemies.

I questioned one of these men and asked him where they were going like that. He replied that he did not know and that none of them knew; but that obviously they must be going somewhere since they were impelled by an irresistible urge to go on.

A curious thing to note: not one of these travelers seemed to resent the ferocious beast hanging around his neck and glued to his back; apparently they considered it a part of themselves. All those worn and serious faces showed not the least sign of despair; under the depressing dome of the sky, with their feet deep in the dust of the earth as desolate as the sky, they went along with the resigned look of men who are condemned to hope forever.

And the procession passed by me and disappeared in the haze of the horizon just where the rounded surface of the planet prevents man's gaze from following.

And for a few moments I persisted in trying to understand this mystery; but soon irresistible Indifference descended upon me, and I was more cruelly oppressed by its weight than those men had been by their crushing Chimeras.

VENUS AND
THE MOTLEY FOOL

WHAT a wonderful day! The vast park lies swooning under the sun's burning eye, like youth under Love's dominion.

Not a sound gives voice to the universal ecstacy of things; even the waters seem to be asleep. Quite unlike human holidays, this is an orgy of silence.

It is as though an ever more luminous light kept making each object glitter with an ever more dazzling splendor; as though the frenzied flowers were trying to rival the azure of the sky by the intensity of their colors, as though the heat, making the perfumes visible, were drawing them up to the sun like smoke.

Yet, in the midst of all this universal joy I caught sight of a grief-stricken soul.

At the feet of a colossal Venus, all of a heap against the pedestal, one of those so-called fools, those voluntary buffoons who, with cap and bells and tricked out in a ridiculous and gaudy costume, are called upon to make kings laugh when they are beset by Boredom or Remorse, raises his tear-filled eyes toward the immortal Goddess.

And his eyes say: "I am the least and the loneliest of men, deprived of love and friendship, wherein I am inferior even to the lowest animals. Yet I, too, am made to understand and to feel immortal Beauty! Ah! Goddess! take pity on my fever and my pain!"

But the implacable Goddess with her marble eyes continues to gaze into the distance, at I know not what.

THE DOG AND THE
SCENT-BOTTLE

COME HERE, my dear, good, beautiful doggie, and smell this excellent perfume which comes from the best perfumer of Paris.

And the dog, wagging his tail, which, I believe, is that poor creature's way of laughing and smiling, came up and put his curious nose on the uncorked bottle. Then, suddenly, he backed away in terror, barking at me reproachfully.

"Ah miserable dog, if I had offered you a package of excrement you would have sniffed at it with delight and perhaps gobbled it up. In this you resemble the public, which should never be offered delicate perfumes that infuriate them, but only carefully selected garbage."

THE BAD GLAZIER

THERE are certain natures, purely contemplative and totally unfit for action, which nevertheless, moved by some mysterious and unaccountable impulse, act at times with a rapidity of which they would never have dreamed themselves capable.

Like the man who, dreading some painful news, instead of going for his mail as usual, cravenly prowls around his concierge's door without daring to go in; or the one who keeps a letter for two weeks without opening it; or the man who only makes up his mind at the end of six months to do something that has urgently needed doing for a year; then, all of a sudden, they feel themselves hurled into action by an irresistible force, like an arrow out of a bow. The moralist and the doctor, who pretend to know everything, are unable to explain how these voluptuous, indolent souls suddenly acquire such a mad energy, or how it is that, although incapable of doing the simplest and most necessary things, they yet discover in themselves at a given moment a lavish courage for performing the most absurd and the most dangerous acts.

One of my friends, the most inoffensive dreamer that ever lived, once set fire to a forest to see, he explained, if it were really as easy to start a fire as people said. Ten times in succession the experiment failed; but the eleventh time it succeeded only too well.

Another will light a cigar standing beside a keg of gunpowder, just *to see, to find out, to test* his luck, to prove to himself he has enough energy to play the gambler, to taste the pleasures of fear, or for no reason at all, through caprice, through idleness.

It is the kind of energy that springs from boredom and day-dreaming; and those who display it so unexpectedly are, in general, as I have said, the most indolent and dreamiest of mortals.

And another man I know, who is so shy that he lowers his eyes even when *men* look at him, so shy that it takes all the poor courage he can muster to enter a café or, at the theatre, to approach the ticket *controlleurs* who seem to him invested with all the majesty of Minos, Iacchus and Radamanthus, will suddenly throw his arms around an old man in the street and kiss him impetuously before the astonished eyes of the passers-by.

Why? Because... because suddenly that particular physiognomy seemed irresistibly appealing? Perhaps; but it would probably be nearer the truth to suppose that he himself has no idea why.

I, too, have more than once been the victim of these outbursts of energy which justify our concluding that some malicious Demon gets into us, forcing us, in spite of ourselves, to carry out his most absurd whims.

One morning I got up feeling out of sorts, sad, and worn out with idleness, and with what seemed to me a compelling urge to do something extraordinary, to perform some brilliant deed. And I opened the window — alas!

(I should like to point out that with certain persons playing practical jokes is not the result of planning or scheming, but a fortuitous inspiration akin, if only because of the compelling force of the impulse, to that humor called hysterical by doctors, satanic by those with more insight than doctors, that drives us toward a multitude of dangerous or improper actions.)

The first person I noticed in the street was a glazier whose piercing and discordant cry floated up to me through the heavy, filthy Paris air. It would be impossible for me to say why I was suddenly seized by an arbitrary loathing for this poor man.

"Hey! Hey!" I shouted, motioning him to come up. And the thought that my room was up six flights of stairs, and that the man must be having a terrible time getting up them with his fragile wares, added not a little to my hilarity.

Finally he appeared. After looking curiously over his panes of glass one by one, I exclaimed: "What! You have no colored glass, no pink, no red, no blue! No magic panes, no panes of Paradise? Scoundrel, what do you mean by going into poor neighborhoods without a single glass to make life beautiful!" And I pushed him, stumbling and grumbling, toward the stairs.

Going out on my balcony I picked up a little flower pot, and when the glazier appeared at the entrance below, I let my engine of war fall down perpendicularly on the edge of his pack. The shock knocked him over and, falling on his back, he succeeded in breaking the rest of his poor ambulatory stock with a shattering noise as of lightning striking a crystal palace.

And drunk with my madness, I shouted down at him furiously: "Make life beautiful! Make life beautiful!"

Such erratic pranks are not without danger and one often has to pay dearly for them. But what is an eternity of damnation compared to an infinity of pleasure in a single second?

ONE O'CLOCK IN THE MORNING

At last! I am alone! Nothing can be heard but the rumbling of a few belated and weary cabs. For a few hours at least silence will be ours, if not sleep. At last! the tyranny of the human face has disappeared, and now there will be no one but myself to make me suffer.

At last! I am allowed to relax in a bath of darkness! First a double turn of the key in the lock. This turn of the key will, it seems to me, increase my solitude and strengthen the barricades that, for the moment, separate me from the world.

Horrible life! Horrible city! Let us glance back over the events of the day: saw several writers, one of them asking me if you could go to Russia by land (he thought Russia was an island, I suppose); disagreed liberally with the editor of a review who to all my objections kept saying: "Here we are on the side of respectability," implying that all the other periodicals were run by rascals; bowed to twenty or more persons of whom fifteen were unknown to me; distributed hand shakes in about the same proportion without having first taken the precaution of buying gloves; to kill time during a shower, dropped in on a dancer who asked me to design her a costume for *Venustre;* went to pay court to a theatrical director who in dismissing me said: "Perhaps you would do well to see Z....; he is the dullest, stupidest and most celebrated of our authors; with him you might get somewhere. Consult him and then we'll see"; boasted (why?) of several ugly things I never did, and cravenly denied some other misdeeds that I had accomplished with the greatest delight; offense of fanfaronnade, crime against human dignity; refused a slight favor to a friend and gave a written recommendation to a perfect rogue; Lord! let's hope that's all!

Dissatisfied with everything, dissatisfied with myself, I long to redeem myself and to restore my pride in the silence and solitude of the night. Souls of those whom I have loved, souls of those whom I have sung, strengthen me, sustain me, keep me from the vanities of the world and its contaminating fumes; and You, dear God! grant me grace to produce a few beautiful verses to prove to myself that I am not the lowest of men, that I am not inferior to those whom I despise.

THE WILD WOMAN
AND THE
FASHIONABLE COQUETTE

"REALLY, my dear, you weary me beyond endurance and I have no pity for you; to hear you sighing one would think you were as miserable as those aged women who toil in the fields, or the old beggar women who pick up crusts at tavern doors.

"If at least your sighs indicated remorse they would be some credit to you; but they mean nothing more than the satiety of gratification and the despondency of too much leisure. And you never cease your useless babble: 'You must love me! I need so to be loved! Comfort me here, caress me there!' But I have an idea which may cure you. For two *sous* and without going very far, there may be a way right in the midst of the fair.

"Now just observe, if you please, this solid iron cage, and see that hairy monster howling like one of the damned, shaking the bars like an orang-utan maddened by exile, imitating to perfection both the circular spring of the tiger, and the stupid posturing of a white bear, and kindly notice that it has a form very vaguely resembling yours.

"This monster is one of those animals generally called 'my angel!'—that is, a woman. The other monster, the one yelling his head off and brandishing a stick, is a husband. He has chained his legitimate spouse as though she were an animal, and displays her at all the street fairs with, of course, the permission of the authorities.

"Now watch carefully! See with what voracity (and not shammed either, perhaps) she tears apart those living rabbits and squalling chickens that her keeper has thrown to her. 'Come, come!' he says, 'one must always keep something for a rainy day!' and with these words of wisdom he cruelly snatches away her prey, the entrails still clinging to the teeth of the ferocious beast—woman, I mean.

"That's it! A good blow of your stick to calm her! For she is darting the most terrific and greedy glances at the pilfered food. Good God! that stick is no stage prop! Did you hear how that whack resounded, in spite of her artificial coat of hair? Moreover, her eyes are starting from her head, and she yells *more naturally* now. The sparks fairly fly from her as from iron on an anvil.

"Such are the conjugal customs of these descendants of Adam and Eve, these works of thy hands, O my God! This woman has certainly the right to complain, although after all, the tittilating delights of fame are perhaps not unknown to her. There are other irremediable misfortunes without such compensations. But in the world into which she has been thrown, it has never occured to her that women deserve a better fate.

"Now what of us, my precious? Seeing the hells with which the world abounds, what do you expect me to think of your pretty little hell, you who lie on stuffs as soft as your own skin, who eat only cooked meat carefully cut for you by a skilled servant?

"And what can they matter to me, all those little sighs swelling your perfumed breast, my hail and hearty coquette? And all those affectations you have learned from books, or that indefatigable melancholy which inspires anything but pity in a spectator. In truth, sometimes I am seized with a desire to teach you what real misfortune is.

"Seeing you like this, my dainty beauty, your feet in the mire and your eyes turned swooningly toward the sky as though waiting for a king, I cannot help thinking of a frog invoking the Ideal. If you despise 'King Log' (that's what I am now, as you very well know), beware of the crane who *will crunch you up,* and *gobble you up,* and *kill you at his pleasure!*

[18]

"Although I may be a poet, I am not such a dupe as you would like to believe, and if you weary me too often with your *precious* whinings, I am going to treat you like the *wild woman,* or else throw you out of the window like an empty bottle."

CROWDS

IT IS NOT given to every man to take a bath of multitude; enjoying a crowd is an art; and only he can relish a debauch of vitality at the expense of the human species, on whom, in his cradle, a fairy has bestowed the love of masks and masquerading, the hate of home, and the passion for roaming.

Multitude, solitude: identical terms, and interchangeable by the active and fertile poet. The man who is unable to people his solitude is equally unable to be alone in a bustling crowd.

The poet enjoys the incomparable privilege of being able to be himself or some one else, as he chooses. Like those wandering souls who go looking for a body, he enters as he likes into each man's personality. For him alone everything is vacant; and if certain places seem closed to him, it is only because in his eyes they are not worth visiting.

The solitary and thoughtful stroller finds a singular intoxication in this universal communion. The man who loves to lose himself in a crowd enjoys feverish delights that the egoist locked up in himself as in a box, and the slothful man like a mollusk in his shell, will be eternally deprived of. He adopts as his own all the occupations, all the joys and all the sorrows that chance offers.

What men call love is a very small, restricted, feeble thing compared with this ineffable orgy, this divine prostitution of the soul giving itself entire, all its poetry and all its charity, to the unexpected as it comes along, to the stranger as he passes.

It is a good thing sometimes to teach the fortunate of this world, if only to humble for an instant their foolish pride, that there are higher joys than theirs, finer and more uncircumscribed. The founders of colonies, shepherds of peoples, missionary priests exiled to the ends of the earth, doubtlessly know something of this mysterious drunkenness; and in the midst of the vast family created by their genius, they must often laugh at those who pity them because of their troubled fortunes and chaste lives.

WIDOWS

VAUVENARGUES says that certain avenues in the public parks are haunted almost exclusively by disappointed ambitions, frustrated inventors, abortive glories, and broken hearts, by all those tumultuous and secret souls still agitated by the last rumblings of the storm, who withdraw as far as possible from the insolent eyes of the gay and the idle. These shady retreats are the meeting places of all those whom life has maimed.

And toward these places poets and philosophers love to direct their avid speculations. There they are sure to find rich pasture. For, as I have said before, they scornfully avoid, above all other places, the ones where the rich and joyous congregate; that trepidation in a void has nothing to attract them. On the contrary, they feel themselves irresistably drawn toward everything that is feeble, destitute, orphaned, and forlorn.

An experienced eye is never mistaken. It can at once decipher in those set or dejected faces, in those eyes, dull and hollow or still shining with the last sparks of struggle, in those deep and numerous wrinkles, in that slow or dislocated gait, the innumerable stories of love deceived, of devotion unrecognized, of effort unrecompensed, of hunger and cold silently endured.

Have you ever noticed widows, poverty-stricken widows, sitting on lonely benches? Whether they are wearing mourning or not they are not difficult to recognize. Moreover, in the mourning of the poor there is invariably something wanting, an absence of consistency that makes it so heartbreaking. The poor are forced to be niggardly with their sorrow. The rich flaunt theirs in all its consummate perfection.

Which is sadder, and more saddening, the widow holding

by the hand a little child with whom she cannot share her thought, or the one who is completely alone? I do not know. . . . I once followed for many hours one of those solitary widows; she held herself stiff and straight in her little threadbare shawl, a stoic pride apparent in her whole bearing.

She was seemingly condemned by her absolute solitude to lead the life of an old bachelor, and this masculine character of her habits added a mysterious piquancy to their austerity. I know not in what miserable eating-place she had lunched, nor how. I followed her into a reading-room and watched her for a long time as she looked through the newspapers with eager eyes — eyes once scalded by bitter tears — searching for something of a passionate and a personal interest.

Finally, in the afternoon, under a lovely autumn sky, one of those skies out of which such a multitude of memories and regrets rain down, she sat on a bench some distance from the crowd, to listen to one of those concerts offered the Parisian public by military bands.

This is probably the little debauch of the innocent old lady (or purified old lady), the well-earned consolation for one of those dull days without a friend, without conversation, without joy, without a soul to confide in, which God, perhaps for many years now, has allowed to descend upon her three hundred and sixty-five times a year.

And another:

I can never help casting a glance, which if not universally sympathetic is at least curious, at the mob of pariahs that crowd around the enclosure of an outdoor concert. The orches-tra pours its festive, martial, or voluptuous airs into the night; glittering gowns trail on the ground; glances cross; the idle, tired of having nothing to do, attitudinize and pretend to be indolently relishing the music. Here nothing that is not rich and happy; nothing that does not breathe forth and inspire indolence and the pleasure of heedlessly living; nothing—except that rabble over there leaning on the outside enclosure, catching a snatch of music gratis at the wind's pleasure, and gazing at the sparkling splendor within.

The reflection of the joys of the rich in the eyes of the poor is always a curious sight. But on this particular day, in that crowd of work blouses and calico dresses, my attention was caught by a figure of such nobility that it stood out in shocking contrast to the environing vulgarity.

This was a tall majestic woman whose whole bearing expressed a nobility such as I cannot remember ever having seen before, not even in the collections of the aristocratic beauties of the past. The odor of proud virtue emanated from her entire person. Her sad, emaciated face was in harmony with the heavy mourning she was wearing. She, too, like the plebeians around her, of whom she took no notice, gazed at that other glittering world with a thoughtful eye, gently nodding her head as she listened to the music.

Strange sight! "Surely," I said to myself, "that is a poverty — if poverty it be — which is incapable of sordid economy; her noble countenance is proof of that. Why then does she choose to stay in a milieu where she offers so conspicuous a contrast?

But drawing nearer to her out of curiosity, I seemed to understand the reason. The tall widow was holding a little boy by the hand who, like herself, was dressed in mourning: the price of admission, no matter how modest, would perhaps be sufficient to pay for one of the child's needs, or preferably for some superfluity — a toy.

And now she will return home on foot, meditating and dreaming, alone, always alone; for a child is turbulent and selfish, without gentleness or patience, and cannot, even less than a simple animal, a dog or a cat, serve as the confidant of lonely sorrows.

THE OLD CLOWN

HOLIDAY crowds swarmed, sprawled, and frolicked everywhere. It was one of those gala days that all the clowns, jugglers, animal trainers, and ambulant hucksters count on, long in advance, to make up for the lean seasons of the year.

On such days people seem to forget everything, all their troubles and their toil; they become like children. For the youngsters it means freedom, the horror of school adjourned for twenty-four hours. For the grown-ups it is an armistice concluded with the malignant forces of the world, a respite from universal struggle and strife.

Even a man of the upper classes, or one engaged in intellectual pursuits, can with difficulty escape the influence of this popular jubilee. They absorb unconsciously their share of this carefree atmosphere. For my part, as a true Parisian, I never fail to visit all the booths that flaunt themselves on these periodic occasions.

And how they vied with one another in fantastic competition! They bawled and they screeched and they bellowed. There was a mixture of cries, crashing brass, and exploding fireworks. Punchinellos and pantaloons, burned by the sun and toughened by wind and rain, made grotesque faces and, with the self-confidence of seasoned actors sure of their effect, shot out their quips and jests and sallies, of a solid and heavy humor akin to Molière's. Strong-men, proud of their monstrous muscles, without forehead or cranium like orang-utans, strutted majestically in their tights that had been washed for the occasion the day before. And dancers, as lovely as fairies or princesses, leaped and pirouetted with the lantern light sparkling in their skirts.

There was nothing but light, dust, shouts, joy, tumult; some spent money, others took it in; and both were equally happy. Little tots tugged at their mothers' skirts begging for candy-sticks, or climbed on their fathers' shoulders to have a better view of a conjuror as dazzling as a god. And dominating all the other odors, the smell of frying fat filled the air like the incense of the fair.

At the end, at the extreme end of the row of booths, as though he had exiled himself in shame from all these splendors, I saw a pitiful old clown, bent, decrepit, the ruin of a man, leaning against one of the posts of his cabin; a cabin more miserable than that of the lowest savage, and in which two candle ends, guttering and smoking, lighted only too well its penury.

Everywhere joy, money-making, debauchery; everywhere the assurance of tomorrow's daily-bread; everywhere frenetic outbursts of vitality. Here absolute misery, and a misery made all the more horrible by being tricked out in comic rags, whose motley contrast was due more to necessity than to art. He was not laughing, the poor wretch! He was not weeping; he was not dancing, he was not gesticulating, he was not shouting; he sang no song, sad or gay, he was soliciting nothing. He was mute and motionless. He had given up, he had abdicated. His fate was sealed.

But with what a profound and unforgettable expression his eyes wandered over the crowds and the lights, the moving flood that stopped just short of his repulsive misery! I felt the terrible hand of hysteria grip my throat, I felt rebellious tears that would not fall, blurring my sight.

What was I to do? Why ask the unhappy man what curiosity, what wonder he had to show in those foul shadows behind his tattered curtain? In truth, I did not dare; and, although you may laugh at my reason, I admit it was because I feared to humiliate him. I had finally decided to leave some money on the platform as I passed, hoping that he would guess my intention, when a sudden surge of the crowd, caused by I know not what disturbance, swept me away from him.

Obsessed by the sight, I looked back, trying to analyze my sudden depression, and I said to myself: "I have just seen the prototype of the old writer who has been the brilliant entertainer of the generation he has outlived, the old poet without friends, without family, without children, degraded by poverty and the ingratitude of the public, and to whose booth the fickle world no longer cares to come!"

CAKE

I WAS traveling. The country around me was of an inexpressible grandeur and sublimity. And I think a little of it must have passed into my soul at that moment. My thoughts leaped with the lightness of the air itself; the vulgar passions, such as hate and profane love, seemed to me now as far away as the clouds that floated in the gorges at my feet; my soul seemed as immense and pure as the enveloping dome of the sky, and earthly things echoed in my memory as faintly as the bells of the invisible herds browsing far, far away on the slopes of another mountain. Over the motionless little lake, jet black from the immensity of its depth, the shadow of a cloud passed occasionally, like the reflection of an airy giant's cloak flying across the sky. And I remember feeling with a joy, mingled with awe, that rare and solemn sensation one has at seeing some great movement evolving without a sound. In short, thanks to the compelling beauty around me, I was at peace with myself and with the universe; in my perfect beatitude and my total forgetfulness of earthly evil, I was beginning to think the newspapers might not be so ridiculous, after all, in wanting to make us believe that man is born good. When, incorrigible matter again making its exigencies felt, I began to think of repairing the fatigue and satisfying the hunger caused by my long climb. I took out of my pocket a thick piece of bread, a leathern cup, and a small bottle of a certain elixir which chemists at that time sold to tourists to be mixed, on occasion, with snow.

I was peacefully cutting my bread when a slight sound made me look up. There in front of me stood a ragged little urchin, dark and disheveled, with hollow eyes that devoured my bread fiercely and, as it seemed to me, pleadingly, and I heard him gasp in a low hoarse voice: "Cake!" I could not help laughing at the appelation with which he thought fit to honor my near-white bread, and I cut off a generous slice and offered it to him. Slowly he came toward me, never taking his eyes off the coveted object; then snatching it out of my hand, he quickly backed away as if he feared that my offer had not been sincere, or that I had already repented it.

But at that moment he was knocked down by another little savage who had sprung from heaven knows where, and so exactly like the first that I took them to be twins. The two of them rolled on the ground struggling for possession of the precious booty, neither willing to share it with the other. Furious, the first clutched the second by the hair; and the second seized one of his brother's ears between his teeth, then, with a superb local oath, spit out a bloody morsel. The legitimate owner of the cake tried to hook his little claws into the usurper's eyes; the latter in turn did his best to choke his adversary with one hand while trying to slip the prize of war into his pocket with the other. But strengthened by despair, the loser struggled to his feet and, butting his head into the other's stomach, sent the victor sprawling on the ground. But why describe the hideous fight which lasted longer than their childish strength had seemed to warrant? The cake traveled from hand to hand and changed pockets at every instant, changing, alas! in size as well, and when finally, exhausted and panting and covered with blood, they stopped from the sheer impossibility of going on, no cause for feud remained; the piece of bread had disappeared, and the crumbs, scattered all around, were indistinguishable from the grains of sand with which they were mingled.

This performance had darkened the landscape, and the calm joy gladdening my soul before the appearance of the two little wretches had completely vanished. Saddened, I sat there for a long time saying over and over to myself: "So there is a superb country where bread is called *cake* and is so rare a delicacy that it is enough to start a war, literally fratricidal!"

THE CLOCK

THE CHINESE can tell the time in the eyes of a cat.

One day a missionary, walking in the suburbs of Nanking, noticed that he had forgotten his watch and asked a little boy the time.

The urchin of the Celestial Empire hesitated at first, then on second thought, replied: "I'll tell you," and disappeared. An instant later he returned with an enormous cat in his arms. He looked it in the eye, as people say, and without a moment's hesitation declared: "It is not quite noon." Which was true.

As for me, when I lean forward to gaze at lovely Féline — so appropriately named — who is at once the honor of her sex, the pride of my heart and the perfume of my mind, whether it be by night or by day, in dazzling light or in deepest shade, always at the back of her adorable eyes I can distinctly see the time, always the same — vast, solemn, wide as space, without minutes and without seconds — a motionless hour not marked on any clock, and yet as airy as a breath, as quick as a glance.

And if some tiresome intruder should come to disturb me while my eyes rest on this delicious dial, if some unmannerly and intolerant Genie, some Demon out of time, should come asking me: "What are you looking at so attentively? What are you looking for in that creature's eyes? Can you tell the time of day in them, idle and prodigal mortal?" I should reply without hesitating: "Yes, I can tell the time; it is Eternity!"

And is this not a really meritorious madrigal, Madam, and just as flamboyant as yourself? Indeed, embroidering this bit of garrish gallantry has given me so much pleasure that I shall ask for nothing in return.

A HEMISPHERE IN YOUR HAIR

LONG, long let me breathe the fragrance of your hair. Let me plunge my face into it like a thirsty man into the water of a spring, and let me wave it like a scented handkerchief to stir memories in the air.

If you only knew all that I see! all that I feel! all that I hear in your hair! My soul voyages on its perfume as other men's souls on music.

Your hair holds a whole dream of masts and sails; it holds seas whose monsoons waft me toward lovely climes where space is bluer and more profound, where fruits and leaves and human skin perfume the air.

In the ocean of your hair I see a harbor teeming with melancholic songs, with lusty men of every nation, and ships of every shape, whose elegant and intricate structures stand out against the enormous sky, home of eternal heat.

In the caresses of your hair I know again the languors of long hours lying on a couch in a fair ship's cabin, cradled by the harbor's imperceptible swell, between pots of flowers and cooling water jars.

On the burning hearth of your hair I breathe in the fragrance of tobacco tinged with opium and sugar; in the night of your hair I see the sheen of the tropic's blue infinity; on the shores of your hair I get drunk with the smell of musk and tar and the oil of cocoanuts.

Long, long, let me bite your black and heavy tresses. When I gnaw your elastic and rebellious hair I seem to be eating memories.

L'INVITATION AU VOYAGE

THERE is a wonderful country, a country of Cocaigne, they say, that I dream of visiting with an old love. A strange country lost in the mists of the North and that might be called the East of the West, the China of Europe, so freely has a warm and capricious fancy been allowed to run riot there, illustrating it patiently and persistantly with an artful and delicate vegetation.

A real country of Cocaigne where everything is beautiful, rich, honest and calm; where order is luxury's mirror; where life is unctuous and sweet to breathe; where disorder, tumult, and the unexpected are shut out; where happiness is wedded to silence; where even the cooking is poetic, rich, and yet stimulating as well; where everything, dear love, resembles you.

You know that feverish sickness which comes over us in our cold despairs, that nostalgia for countries we have never known, that anguish of curiosity? There is a country that resembles you, where everything is beautiful, rich, honest and calm, where fancy has built and decorated an Occidental China, where life is sweet to breathe, where happiness is wedded to silence. It is there we must live, it is there we must die.

Yes, it is there we must go to breathe, to dream, and to prolong the hours in an infinity of sensations. A musician has written *l'Invitation à la valse*; who will write *l'Invitation au voyage* that may be offered to the beloved, to the chosen sister?

Yes, in such an atmosphere it would be good to live — where there are more thoughts in slower hours, where clocks strike happiness with a deeper, a more significant solemnity.

On shining panels or on darkly rich and gilded leathers, discreet paintings repose, as deep, calm and devout as the souls of the painters who depicted them. Sunsets throw their glowing colors on the walls of dining-room and drawing-room, sifting softly through lovely hangings or intricate high windows with mullioned panes. All the furniture is immense, fantastic, strange, armed with locks and secrets like all civilized souls. Mirrors, metals, fabrics, pottery, and works of the goldsmith's art play a mute mysterious symphony for the eye, and every corner, every crack, every drawer and curtain's fold breathes forth a curious perfume, a perfume of Sumatra whispering *come back,* which is the soul of the abode.

A true country of Cocaigne, I assure you, where everything is rich, shining and clean like a good conscience or well-scoured kitchen pots, like chiseled gold or variegated gems! All the treasures of the world abound there, as in the house of a laborious man who has put the whole world in his debt. A singular country and superior to all others, as art is superior to Nature who is there transformed by dream, corrected, remodeled and adorned.

Let them seek and seek again, let them endlessly push back the limits of their happiness, those horticultural Alchemists! Let them offer prizes of sixty, a hundred thousand florins for the solution of their ambitious problems! As for me, I have found my *black tulip,* I have found my *blue dahlia!*

Incomparable flower, rediscovered tulip, allegorical dahlia, it is there, is it not, in that beautiful country, so calm, so full of dream, that you must live, that you must bloom? Would you not there be framed within your own analogy, would you not see yourself reflected there in your own *correspondence,* as the mystics say?

Dreams! Always dreams! And the more ambitious and delicate the soul, all the more impossible the dreams. Every man possesses his own dose of natural opium, ceaselesly secreted and renewed, and from birth to death how many hours can we reckon of positive pleasure, of successful and decided action? Shall we ever live in, be part of, that picture my imagination has painted, and that resembles you?

These treasures, these furnishings, this luxury, this order, these perfumes, and these miraculous flowers, they are you! And you are the great rivers too, and the calm canals. And those great ships that they bear along laden with riches and from which rise the sailors' rhythmic chants, they are my thoughts that sleep or that rise on the swells of your breast. You lead them gently toward the sea which is the Infinite, as you mirror the sky's depth in the crystalline purity of your soul; — and when, weary with rolling waters and surfeited with the spoils of the Orient, they return to their port of call, still they are my thoughts coming back, enriched, from the Infinite to you.

THE POOR CHILD'S TOY

I SHOULD LIKE to offer a suggestion for an innocent diversion. There are so few amusements that are not culpable!

When you go out in the morning with the settled idea of rambling over the highways, fill your pockets with little penny devices such as those flat puppets manipulated by a single string, a blacksmith hammering on an anvil, a knight on a horse whose tail is a whistle, and outside the taverns and under the trees offer them as gifts to all the unknown poor children you may meet. You will see their eyes open unbelievably wide. At first they won't dare to take them; they won't believe in their good fortune. Then their hands will clutch the present eagerly, and they will run away like cats who go far off to eat any morsel you give them, having learned to be wary of men.

Behind the iron gate of an immense garden, at the back of which could be seen a charming chateau gleaming whitely in the sun, stood a beautiful, blooming little boy smartly dressed in country togs that are always so enchanting.

Luxury, carefree days, and the habitual spectacle of abundance make such children so lovely that they seem to be made of a different clay from the children of the moderately, and the very poor.

Beside him on the grass lay a magnificent toy, as blooming as its master, gilded and shining, dressed in purple, and covered with plumes and glittering beads. But the child was paying no attention to his favorite toy, and this is what he was looking at:

On the other side of the gate on the highway, standing in the midst of nettles and thistles, was another child, pitifully black and grimy, one of those urchin-pariahs whose beauty an impartial eye would discover if, as the eye of a connoisseur detects an authentic master under the coachmaker's varnish, it peeled off the disgusting patina of poverty.

Through the symbolic bars separating two worlds, highroad and mansion, the poor child was showing the rich child his own toy, which the latter was scrutinizing breathlessly, as though it had been some rare and unheard of object. Well, this toy that the grimy little brat was shaking, teetering and turning in a box covered with wire, was a living rat! The parents out of economy, I suppose, had taken the toy from nature itself.

And the two children were laughing together like brothers, with teeth of *identical* whiteness.

THE FAIRIES' GIFTS

GRAND ASSEMBLY of the Fairies, gathered together to effect the distribution of gifts among the new-born infants who had come into the world in the last twenty-four hours.

All these ancient and capricious Sisters of Destiny, these strange mothers of joy and sorrow, were very different from one another; some were sad and surly, others had a mad, mischievous gaiety; some were young and had always been young, others were old and had always been old.

All the fathers who believed in Fairies had come to the assembly with their infants in their arms.

Talents, Faculties, good Fortunes, invincible Conjunctures were piled up beside the tribunal, for all the world like commencement-day prizes. But the difference was that these Gifts were not the recompense for any effort but, on the contrary, a favor accorded to a person who has not yet lived, a favor capable of deciding his destiny and of becoming either the cause of his misfortune or the source of all his happiness.

The poor Fairies were in a pother; for there was a very large crowd of petitioners, and the intermediary world, situated between man and God, is subject, just as ours is, to the law of Time and all his infinite progeny, the Days, the Hours, the Minutes, the Seconds.

In truth, they were as flurried as one of the ministers of state on his audience day, or the employees of a pawn-shop when a national holiday authorizes the redemption of pledges gratis. I even think they glanced at the clock with as much impatience as human judges who have been sitting on the bench all day and cannot help longing for their dinners, their wives and their beloved bed-room slippers. If in supernatural justice there is some precipitancy and confusion, we ought not to be too surprised to find them, at times, in human justice as well. Otherwise we ourselves would be unjust judges.

And so it happened on that day, a few blunders were committed which might be looked upon as odd if prudence, rather than caprice, were the distinctive and eternal characteristic of the Fairies.

Thus the magnetic power of attracting wealth was awarded to the heir of an immensely rich family, and as he had not been endowed with a sense of charity or the least covetousness for the good things of this world, he was sure to find himself terribly embarrassed by his millions later on.

Thus also, the love of Beauty, and poetic Power, were awarded to the son of a pitiful pauper, a stone quarrier by trade, who could in no way either advance the talents, or alleviate the needs of his deplorable offspring.

I have forgotten to say that the distribution on these solemn occasions is without appeal, and that no gift may be refused.

Thinking their task accomplished, all the Fairies had risen, for not a single gift was left, no bounty remained to throw to this human horde, when a worthy man, a poor little shopkeeper, I fancy, sprang forward, and catching hold of the multicolored vapor gown of the nearest Fairy, cried:

"But, Madam! You have forgotten us! What about my baby? I hate to think I've made the trip for nothing."

The Fairy might well have been discountenanced; for there was *nothing* left. Happily, she remembered in time a well-known, though rarely applied, law of the supernatural world — the world inhabited by impalpable deities who, being friends of man, must often adapt themselves to his human passions, such as the Fairies, Gnomes, Salamanders, Sylphids, Sylphs, Nixies, and Undines (male and female) — I refer to the law that, in such a case as the present when gifts run short, gives a Fairy the power to accord one more gift, provided she has imagination enough to create one on the spot.

[38]

So the good Fairy replied with a self-possession worthy of her rank: "I bestow upon your son . . . I bestow upon him —the *Gift of pleasing.*"

"Pleasing? But pleasing how? Pleasing why?" asked the obstinate little shop-keeper who was doubtlessly one of those reasoners, only too common, who is incapable of rising to the logic of the Absurd.

"Because! Just because!" replied the incensed Fairy, turning her back on him.

Rejoining the cohort of Fairies, she said: "What do you think of that vain little Frenchman? He insists upon understanding everything, and even after he has obtained the best gift of the lot for his son, he still dares to question, and to dispute the Indisputable."

THE TEMPTATIONS
OR
EROS, PLUTOS AND FAME

LAST NIGHT two superb Satans, and a not less extraordinary
Sataness, climbed the mysterious stairs up which Hell launches
its assaults on the weakness of sleeping man, and communicates
with him in secret. Gloriously they stood before me, like actors
on a stage. A sulphurous splendor emanated from the three
personnages thus standing out in relief against the dense back-
ground of the night. They looked so proud, with so imperious
an air, that at first I mistook them for real gods.

The countenance of the first Satan was of an ambiguous
sex, and in the lines of his body too, there was the same soft-
ness that the ancients were wont to give to Bacchus. His beauti-
ful languid eyes, shadowy and vague in color, resembled violets
that are still heavy with the tears of storm, while his half open
lips were like warm censers exhaling the agreeable odor of
perfumeries, and whenever he sighed, musky insects flitting
about were illuminated in the fiery glow of his breath.

Around his purple tunic, like a girdle twined an iridescent
serpent that lifted its head and turned toward him with lan-
guorous live-ember eyes. And suspended from this living girdle,
alternating with vials of sinister cordials, hung shining knives
and surgical instruments.

In his right hand he held another vial whose content was
of a luminous red, and which bore these curious words upon
its label: "Drink my blood, a perfect cordial"; in his left, a
violin which he used, no doubt, to sing his pleasures and his

pains, and to spread the contagion of his madness on witches'-sabbath nights.

A few links of a broken golden chain dragged at his delicate ankles and, when they hampered him and forced him to look down, vain as he was, he never failed to admire his brilliant toe nails as highly polished as precious gems.

He looked at me with his inconsolably sad eyes, filled with an insidious intoxication, and said in a melodious voice: "If you wish, if you wish, I will make you the master of living matter, as the sculptor is of clay, but an incomparably greater master; and you shall know the pleasure, constantly renewed, of escaping from yourself to forget yourself in another being, and of attracting to yourself other souls to lose themselves in yours."

And I answered him: "Thank you, no! I want none of your human wares that are probably no better than my own poor self. And although remembering makes me more or less ashamed, I still have no desire to forget a thing; and even if I did not recognize you, you old monster, your mysterious cutlery, your dubious vials, and the chains shackling your feet are symbols that demonstrate clearly enough the disadvantages of friendship with you. You may keep your gifts."

The second Satan had nothing of that tragic and, at the same time, smiling air, nor those insinuating manners, nor that exquisite perfumed beauty. He was a man of vast proportions, with an eyeless countenance. His heavy paunch hung down over his thighs, and his skin was gilded and illustrated, as though tattooed all over, with masses of little hurrying figures, representing numerous forms of universal misery. There were lean little men who had hung themselves from nails, there were deformed skinny little gnomes whose supplicating eyes begged more eloquently for alms than their trembling hands: and there were old mothers with premature infants clinging to their wasted breasts, and there were plenty of others too.

The gigantic Satan tapped his immense belly with his fist, and there came from it a prolonged metallic jingling that ended in a vague groaning, as of many human voices. And he laughed, indecently displaying his decayed teeth, a great imbecilic laugh like that of certain men in every country after they have dined too well.

And this one said to me: "I can give you the thing that will procure you everything else; that is worth everything else; that takes the place of everything else!" And he tapped his monstrous belly whose sonorous echo was a fit commentary on his vulgar offer.

I turned away in disgust as I replied: "I do not need other peoples' misery for my enjoyment, and I want none of your wealth, ghastly with all the misfortunes that your skin, like a wall paper, displays."

As for the Sataness, I should be lying if I failed to admit that at first glance she seemed to me to have a singular charm. And I can find no better way of defining this charm than by comparing it to that of certain women past their prime but who will never grow old, and whose beauty seems to hold some of the poignant magic of old ruins. She had an imperious and yet unbridled air, and her eyes, although marked by the years, still held all their power of fascination. What struck me particularly was the mysterious quality of her voice reminding me of all the loveliest *contralti* I had ever heard, and also of the huskiness of throats too often washed with *aqua vitae*.

"Would you like a proof of my power?" said the false goddess in her paradoxically seductive voice. "Listen."

And she sounded an enormous trumpet, having long streamers like one of those rustic pipes, that bore the names of all the newspapers of the world, and on this trumpet she cried my name, which went rolling through space with the noise of a thousand thunderbolts. And its echo came back to me, reverberated from the farthest planet.

"The Devil!" I said, half won over. "Now that is something!" But on examining this seductive fury more closely, I seemed to remember having seen her before somewhere drinking with some of my acquaintances, and the hoarse sound of the brass brought back to my ears a vague recollection of another prostituted trumpet I had heard.

So with all my scorn I replied: "Away with you! I am not one to marry the mistress of a certain person I do not care to name."

Of such courageous self-denial I surely had the right to be proud. But unhappily when I awoke all my fortitude forsook me. "In truth," I said to myself, "I must have been sound asleep indeed to have displayed such scruples. Ah! if only they would come again while I am awake, I would certainly not be so squeamish."

And I called on them aloud, begging them to forgive me, promising to degrade myself as often as should be necessary to win their favor. But I must surely have mortally offended them, for they have never returned.

XXII

EVENING TWILIGHT

DAYLIGHT fades. A great peace descends into poor minds that the day's work has wearied; and thoughts take on the tender and shadowy tints of twilight.

Yet, through the transparent clouds of evening, a great clamor from the top of the mountain reaches me on my balcony, a confusion of discordant cries transformed by distance into a desolate harmony, like that of the rising tide or impending storm.

Who are these hapless ones to whom evening brings no solace, to whom, like the owls, the approach of night is the signal for a witches'-sabbath? This sinister ululation comes to me from the black mad-house perched on the mountain; as I smoke my evening pipe, contemplating the peace of the immense valley bristling with houses, whose windows say: "Here is peace; here is a happy family!" I can, when the wind blows from up there, cradle my wondering fancy on this imitation of the harmonies of hell.

Twilight excites madmen. I remember two of my friends who always became ill at dusk. One of them would lose all sense of the obligations of friendship and of ordinary courtesy, and would fly at the first comer like a savage. I have seen him throw an excellent chicken at a head-waiter because he imagined he saw in it some hieroglyphic insult. For him evening, that herald of all voluptuous pleasures, spoiled all things, even the most succulent.

The other, a prey to disappointed ambition, as daylight waned, began to grow bitter, gloomy and quarrelsome. Still indulgent and sociable by day, he was pitiless at night; and would vent furiously, not only on others but on himself as well, all his crepuscular spleen.

The former died insane, unable to recognize his wife and child; the latter is still tortured by a perpetual disquietude and even if all the honors that republics and princes can confer were now heaped upon his head, I believe that twilight would still quicken in him a feverish craving for imaginary distinctions. Night, which filled their minds with its own darkness, brings light to mine; and although it is not rare to observe the same cause bringing about contrary results, it never fails to perplex and to alarm me.

O night! O refreshing darkness! to me you are the signal for an inner feast, my deliverer from anguish! In the solitude of the plain, in the stony labyrinths of the metropolis, scintillation of stars, bright bursts of city lights, you are the fireworks of my goddess Liberty!

Twilight, how sweet you are, how tender! The rosy glow lingering on the horizon like the last agony of day conquered by victorious night; the flames of the candelabra making dull red splashes against the sunset's dying glory; the heavy draperies that some unseen hand draws out of the depth of the East — it all seems to imitate those complex sentiments that at life's most solemn moments war with each other in man's heart.

Or it may remind one of those curious costumes dancers wear, that reveal under dark transparent gauze the muted splendors of a dazzling skirt, just as the delicious past shines through the somber present; and the gold and silver stars sprinkled over it, represent the fires of fancy that shine brightly only in the deep mourning of the night.

XXIII

SOLITUDE

A PHILANTHROPIC journalist says that solitude is bad for man-kind; and he supports his proposition, like all unbelievers, with citations from the Church Fathers.

I know that the wilderness is a favorite haunt of the Devil and that the Spirit of lubricity is kindled in lonely places. But it is possible that this solitude is dangerous only for those idle and vagrant souls who people it with their own passions and chimeras.

Certainly a garrulous man, whose chief pleasure in life is to declaim from pulpit or rostrum, would run the risk of becoming a raving maniac on Robinson Crusoe's island. I do not insist on my journalist having all the virtues and the courage of Crusoe. But I do object to his directing his imputation against the lovers of solitude and mystery.

Chattering humanity is full of individuals who would face the death penalty with less horror if, from the top of the scaffold, they were permitted to make a mighty harangue with no fear of an untimely interruption from the drums of Santerre.

I do not pity them, since I feel that their oratorical effusions procure them pleasures quite equal to those which others derive from silence and self-communion; but I despise them.

All I ask of my cursed journalist is to be allowed to amuse myself in my own way. "And so," he says with his most evan-gelical and nasal inflection, "you never feel the need of sharing your pleasures?" Ah, the subtle envy! He knows that I scorn his pleasures and he tries to insinuate himself into mine, the odious kill-joy!

"That great misfortune of not being able to be alone! . . ."

says La Bruyère somewhere, as though to shame those who have to go into crowds to forget themselves, doubtless fearing that they could not endure themselves alone.

"Almost all our ills come from not staying in our own room," says another wise man, I believe it was Pascal, recalling from his cell of self-communion all those madmen who seek happiness in activity and in what I might call, to use the wonderful language of the day, the *brotherhood* of prostitution.

XXIV

PROJECTS

HE SAID to himself as he walked through a great lonely park: "How beautiful she would be in one of those gorgeous and elaborate court costumes, as, in the soft evening air, she descended the marble stairs of a palace facing broad lawns and lakes! For by nature she has the air of a princess.

Later, passing through a little street he stopped in front of a print shop, and looking through a portfolio and finding a picture of a tropical scene, he thought: "No! it is not in a palace that I should like to cherish her dear life. We should never feel *at home* in one. Besides there would be no place on those gold encrusted walls to hang her portrait; and in those formal halls there is never an intimate corner. Decidedly *here* I have found the place in which to live and cultivate the dream of my life."

And while his eyes continued to examine every detail of the print, he went on musing: "A lovely wooden cabin by the sea and all around those curious glossy trees whose names I have forgotten ... in the air an indefinable, an intoxicating fragrance ... in the cabin the heavy scent of musk and roses ... and farther, behind our little domain, the tops of masts rocking on the waves ... all around us, beyond our bedroom with its shutters softening the glare to a rosy glow, and decorated with cool mats and heady flowers and Portuguese rococo chairs of heavy somber wood (where she will sit so calmly and well fanned, smoking her slightly opiumed tobacco), and beyond the veranda, the twittering of birds drunk with the sun and the chattering of little negro girls ... while at night, as an accompaniment to my dreams, the plaintive song of the music-trees, the melancholy *filaos!* Yes, truly this is the setting I have been looking for. What do I want of a palace?"

And a little farther on, as he was walking along a wide avenue, he noticed a cozy little inn, and in the window, gay with curtains of striped calico, two laughing faces. And instantly: "Really," he cried, "what a vagabond my mind must be to go looking so far afield for pleasure that is so near at hand. Pleasure and happiness are to be found in the first inn you come to, any chance inn teeming with delights. A great wood fire, gaudy crockery, a passable supper, a vigorous wine, and a very wide bed with sheets, a little coarse, but cool; what could be better?"

And going home at that hour of the day when Wisdom's counsels are not silenced by the roar of the outside world, he said to himself: "I have possessed three homes today, and was equally happy in all of them. Why should I drive my body from place to place, when my soul travels so lightly? And why carry out one's projects, since the project is sufficient pleasure in itself?"

XXV

THE BEAUTIFUL DOROTHEA

THE SUN overwhelms the city with its perpendicular and fulminating rays; the sand is blinding and the sea glitters. The stupified world weakly succumbs and takes its siesta, a siesta that is a sort of delicious death in which the sleeper, between sleeping and waking, tastes all the voluptuous delight of annihilation.

Meanwhile Dorothea, strong and proud as the sun, walks along the deserted street, the only living thing at this hour under the blue, a shining black spot in the sunlight.

She walks, swaying gently from such a slender waist set on such generous hips! Her pale pink dress of clinging silk makes a lovely contrast with the darkness of her skin, and molds accurately her long bust, the curve of her back and her pointed breasts.

A red parasol, shading her from the sun, rouges her dusky face with its blood-red glow.

The weight of the enormous pile of hair that is almost blue, pulls back her delicate head and gives her an indolently triumphant air. And the heavy ear-rings keep chattering secrets in her pretty ears.

From time to time the sea breeze lifts a corner of her flowing skirt, revealing a superb and glistening leg; and her foot, like the feet of the marble goddesses that Europe keeps carefully shut up in museums, imprints its image faithfully on the fine sand. For Dorothea is such a prodigious coquette that the pleasure of being admired prevails with her over the pride of no longer being a slave, and although freed, she still goes barefoot.

Thus she harmoniously takes her way, happy to be alive, and smiling her white smile as though she saw in the distance ahead of her a mirror reflecting her beauty and proud carriage.

At an hour when even the dogs groan with pain under the gnawing teeth of the sun, what invincible motive brings lazy Dorothea abroad, as beautiful and cool as bronze?

Why has she left her little cabin so coquettishly arranged, whose mats and flowers make such a perfect boudoir at so small a cost; where she loves to sit and comb her hair, to smoke and to be fanned by those great feather fans, or to gaze into her mirror, while the sea, pounding the shore not a hundred feet away, serves as a powerful and rhythmic accompaniment to her vague day-dreams, and exciting, aromatic odors come to her from the back of the court-yard where a ragout of saffroned rice and crabs is cooking in an iron pot?

Perhaps she has a rendezvous with some young officer who, on distant shores, has heard his comrades talking of the famous Dorothea. She would ask him, of course, to describe the Opera Ball, and also, the simple creature, if one could go to it barefoot as to Sunday dances here, when even the old Kafir women get drunk and delirious with pleasure; and if all the beautiful Paris ladies are more beautiful than she?

Dorothea is admired and pampered, and she would be perfectly happy if only she were not obliged to save up, *piastre* by *piastre*, enough to free her little sister who is all of eleven years old, and mature already, and so beautiful! She will doubtless succeed, the kindly Dorothea: but the child's master is too miserly to understand any beauty other than the beauty of his *écus*.

XXVI

THE EYES OF THE POOR

AH! So YOU would like to know why I hate you today? It will certainly be harder for you to understand than for me to explain, for you are, I believe, the most perfect example of feminine impermeability that exists.

We had spent a long day together which to me had seemed short. We had duly promised each other that all our thoughts should be shared in common, and that our two souls henceforth be but one — a dream which, after all, has nothing original about it except that, although dreamed by every man on earth, it has been realized by none.

That evening, a little tired, you wanted to sit down in front of a new café forming the corner of a new boulevard still littered with rubbish but that already displayed proudly its unfinished splendors. The café was dazzling. Even the gas burned with all the ardor of a début, and lighted with all its might the blinding whiteness of the walls, the expanse of mirrors, the gold cornices and moldings, fat-cheeked pages dragged along by hounds on leash, laughing ladies with falcons on their wrists, nymphs and goddesses bearing on their heads piles of fruits, *patés* and game, Hebes and Ganymedes holding out little amphoras of syrups or parti-colored ices; all history and all mythology pandering to gluttony.

On the street directly in front of us, a worthy man of about forty, with tired face and greying beard, was standing holding a small boy by the hand and carrying on his arm another little thing, still too weak to walk. He was playing nurse-maid, taking the children for an evening stroll. They were in rags. The three faces were extraordinarily serious, and those six eyes stared fixedly at the new café with admiration, equal in degree but differing in kind according to their ages.

The eyes of the father said: "How beautiful it is! How beautiful it is! All the gold of the poor world must have found its way onto those walls." The eyes of the little boy: "How beautiful it is! How beautiful it is! But it is a house where only people who are not like us can go." As for the baby, he was much too fascinated to express anything but joy — utterly stupid and profound.

Song writers say that pleasure ennobles the soul and softens the heart. The song was right that evening as far as I was concerned. Not only was I touched by this family of eyes, but I was even a little ashamed of our glasses and decanters, too big for our thirst. I turned my eyes to look into yours, dear love, to read *my* thought in them; and as I plunged my eyes into your eyes, so beautiful and so curiously soft, into those green eyes, home of Caprice and governed by the Moon, you said: "Those people are insufferable with their great saucer eyes. Can't you tell the proprietor to send them away?"

So you see how difficult it is to understand one another, my dear angel, how incommunicable thought is, even between two people in love.

XXVII

A HEROIC DEATH

FANCIOULLE was an admirable buffoon and almost like one of the Prince's friends. But for men whose profession it is to be funny, serious things have a fatal attraction, and one day, although it may seem strange that ideas of patriotism and liberty should take despotic possession of a mummer's brain, Fancioulle joined a conspiracy formed by certain discontented nobles of the court.

There exist everywhere worthy men always ready to denounce their more atrabiliar brothers who long to dethrone princes and, without bothering to consult it, to reconstitute society. The nobles in question were arrested as well as Fancioulle, and all of them faced certain death.

I could readily believe that the Prince was quite put out to find his favorite player among the rebels. The Prince was neither better nor worse than other men; but having an excessive sensibility he was in general far more cruel than his fellows. A passionate lover of the fine arts, as well as an excellent connoisseur, he was an altogether insatiable voluptuary. Indifferent enough in regard to men and morals, himself a real artist, he dreaded one enemy only, Boredom; and the extravagant efforts he made to vanquish or to outwit this tyrant of the world, would most certainly have won him the epithet of "monster" from a severe historian, if in the Prince's dominions any one had been permitted to write anything whatever which did not make exclusively for pleasure or for astonishment, one of pleasure's most delicate forms. The misfortune of the Prince was in not having a stage vast enough for his genius. There are young Neros, stifled in too narrow bounds, whose names and good intentions will forever remain unknown to future generations. A heedless Providence had given this Prince faculties greater than his domains.

Suddenly a rumor spread that the sovereign had decided to pardon all the conspirators; and the origin of this rumor was an announcement that a magnificent pantomime was to be given in which Fancioulle would play one of his most famous, one of his most successful roles, and at which even the condemned nobles, it was said, were to be present; an evident proof, added superficial minds, of the generous proclivities of the offended Prince.

On the part of a man so naturally and deliberately eccentric, anything was possible, even virtue, even clemency, especially if in it he could hope to find some unexpected pleasures. But for those who, like myself, had probed deeper into that curious sick soul, it was infinitely more probable that the Prince wanted to test the value of the histrionic talent of a man condemned to die. He wanted to profit by this occasion to make a physiological experiment of a *capital* interest, to find out to what extent an artist's faculties might be changed or modified in a situation as extraordinary as this; beyond that, was there in his mind, perhaps, a more or less definite idea of mercy? This is a point that has never been clarified.

At last, the great day having arrived, this little court displayed all its pomps; and it would be difficult to conceive, unless one had seen it, what incredible splendor the privileged class of a tiny state with limited resources, was able to muster for a notable occasion. This one was doubly so by the wonder of the luxury displayed as well as by the mysterious moral interest attaching to it.

Sieur Fancioulle excelled especially in silent parts or ones with few words, which are often the principle roles in those fairy pantomimes whose object is to represent symbolically the mystery of life. He came out lightly onto the stage, with a perfect ease that confirmed the noble audience in its notion of clemency and pardon.

When people say of an actor: "What a good actor," they are using an expression which implies that beneath the character they can still distinguish the actor, that is to say, art, effort, volition. But if an actor should succeed in being, in relation to the part he played, what the best statues of antiquity, if miraculously animated they lived, walked and saw, would be in relation to the general, the confused idea of beauty, that would indeed be a singular case and altogether unheard of. Fancioulle was that night just such a perfect idealization, so that one could not help believing in the impersonation as alive, possible and real. The buffoon came and went, laughed and wept, and lashed into fury, with always about his head an imperishable aureole, invisible to all, but visible to me, that blended in a strange amalgam the beams of Art and the glory of Martyrdom. Fancioulle, by what special grace I cannot say, introduced something of divine and supernatural into his most extravagant buffooneries. My pen trembles and tears of an emotion that has never left me, fill my eyes, while I look for words to describe for you that unforgettable evening. Fancioulle proved to me in the most peremptory, the most irrefutable way, that the intoxication of Art is more apt than any other to veil the terrors of the eternal abyss; and that genius can play a part, even on the edge of the grave, with such joy that it does not see the grave, lost, as it is, in a paradise that shuts out all thought of death and destruction.

The whole audience, blasé and frivolous though they were, soon fell under the all-powerful sway of the artist. No thought remained of death, of mourning, or of punishment. Every one gave himself up without a qualm to the voluptuous and multitudinous pleasures the sight of a masterpiece of living art affords. Explosions of delight and admiration again and again reverberated to the vaults of the edifice with the noise of a continuous thunder. The Prince himself, in a frenzy of intoxication, joined in the applause of his court.

However, for a discerning eye, this intoxication was not without alloy. Did he feel himself cheated in his despotic power, humiliated in his art of striking terror into hearts and chill into souls, frustrated in his hopes, flouted in his forecasts? Such suppositions, not altogether justified yet not unjustifiable, ran through my mind while I watched the Prince's face, as over his habitual palor, a new palor spread like snow falling upon snow. His lips were more and more tightly compressed and his eyes blazed with an inner fire resembling that of jealousy or spite, even while he ostensibly applauded his former friend, the strange buffoon who now played death's buffoon so superbly. At a certain moment I saw his Highness turn toward a little page standing behind him, and whisper in his ear. A roguish smile flashed across the child's charming face; and he left the royal box as if to carry out some urgent commission.

A few minutes later a shrill prolonged hiss broke in upon Fancioulle in one of his greatest moments, rending all ears and hearts. And from that part of the hall whence this unexpected rebuff had come, a child darted out into a corridor with stifled laughter.

Fancioulle, awakened from his dream, closed his eyes, and when almost at once he opened them again, they seemed to have grown inordinately large, then he opened his mouth as though struggling for breath, staggered forward a step, then backward, and fell dead upon the stage.

Had the hiss, swift as a sword, really frustrated the hangman? Had the Prince foreseen the homicidal eventuality of his ruse? There is ground for doubt. Did he regret his cherished, his inimitable Fancioulle? It is sweet and legitimate to hope so.

The guilty nobles had enjoyed the delights of the theatre for the last time. The same night they were effaced from life.

Since then several other mimes, justly appreciated in many countries, have come to the court of * * * but none has ever been able to approach the miraculous talent of Fancioulle, nor to rise to the same *favor*.

XXVIII

COUNTERFEIT

As WE WERE leaving the tobacconist's I saw my friend carefully separating his money; in the left pocket of his waistcoat he slipped all the gold pieces; in the right, the silver; in his left trouser pocket he put a handful of pennies, and finally in the right, after the most careful scrutiny, a two-franc piece.

"What a singularly minute distribution," I said to myself.

Soon we passed a beggar who held out his cap to us with a trembling hand. For the man of feeling who is able to read them, I know nothing more distressing than the mute eloquence of a pauper's pleading eyes, so full of humility and reproach. There is in them something of the profound and complex emotion to be seen in the tear-filled eyes of a dog being beaten.

My friend's offering was considerably larger than mine, and I said to him: "You are right; next to feeling surprise oneself, there is no greater pleasure than giving someone else a surprise." "It was counterfeit," he replied tranquilly as though to justify his prodigality.

But in my miserable brain, which is forever flying off at a tangent (what an exhausting faculty nature has given me!), the idea suddenly occurred to me that such conduct in my friend was only excusable if it came from a desire of bringing some excitement into the poor devil's life, perhaps even of learning all the different consequences, disastrous or otherwise, that a counterfeit coin in the hands of a beggar, might engender. Might it not multiply into many pieces of good money? Might it not also lead to prison? A baker, a tavern keeper, for instance, might have him arrested as a counterfeiter or a disseminator of bad money. But on the other hand, the counterfeit coin for a poor little speculator, might well be the germ of several days' wealth. And so my fancy ran riot, lending wings to my friend's imagination and drawing all possible deductions from all possible hypotheses.

But he rudely shattered my reverie by repeating my own words: "Yes, you are right, there is no sweeter pleasure than to surprise a man by giving him more than he expects."

I looked him squarely in the eye, and I was appalled to see that his eyes shone with unquestionable candor. I understood perfectly then that his object had been to perform a charitable deed while making a good speculation; to gain forty *sols* and God's heart at the same time, and to win paradise economically; in short, to carry off gratis a certificate of charity. I could almost have forgiven him his desire for the reprehensible enjoyment I had just been supposing him capable of; I should have found something curious, arresting in his desire to compromise paupers; but I will never pardon him the ineptitude of his calculation. To be mean is never excusable, but there is some virtue in knowing that one is; the unforgivable vice is to do harm out of stupidity.

XXIX

THE GENEROUS GAMBLER

YESTERDAY on the crowded boulevard, I felt myself jostled by a mysterious Being whom I have always longed to know, and although I had never seen him before, I recognized him at once. He must have felt a similar desire in regard to me, for as he passed he gave me a knowing wink which I was quick to obey. I followed him closely and soon, still at his heels, descended into a magnificent subterranean dwelling of a fabulous luxury beyond anything the upper habitations of Paris could boast. And it seemed to me odd that I should have passed this enchanting haunt so often without suspecting that here was the entrance. The exquisite, though heady, atmosphere of the place made one instantaneously forget all the tedious horrors of life; here one breathed a somber beatitude similar to that which the lotus-eaters must have felt when, landing on the enchanted isle bathed in the light of an eternal afternoon, and hearing the soothing sound of melodious cascades, they suddenly longed never to see their penates again, their wives and children, never again to venture forth over the towering waves of the sea.

Here were strange faces of men and women who were marked with the sign of fatal beauty, and I seemed to remember having seen them before, but at what period or in what countries it was impossible to recall; they inspired in me a fraternal sympathy rather than that apprehension commonly aroused by the sight of anything alien. If I were to attempt to give some idea of the singular expression of their eyes I should say that I have never seen eyes that shone so fiercely with the horror of boredom and with the immortal longing to feel themselves live.

By the time my host and I were seated, we were already firm

friends. We ate; we drank immoderately of all sorts of extraordinary wines, and no less extraordinary was the fact that even after several hours it seemed to me that I was no more drunk than he. But gaming, that superhuman pleasure, had interrupted, at divers intervals, our frequent libations, and I should also say that, with perfect nonchalance and heroic heedlessness, I had played and lost my soul in a binding pact. The soul is a thing so impalpable, often so useless, and sometimes so in the way, that I felt somewhat less emotion over its loss than if I had dropped my visiting card out walking.

Slowly we smoked several cigars whose incomparable taste and aroma made the soul homesick for countries and pleasures it had never known, and drunk with all these delights, in an access of familiarity that did not seem to displease him, I had the temerity to exclaim as I lifted my brimming glass: "To your immortal health, Old Harry!"

We talked of the universe, of its creation and of its final destruction; of the big idea of the century, that is, the idea of progress and perfectability, and in general of all forms of human infatuation. On this subject His Highness was never at a loss for gay and irrefutable ironies, and he expressed himself with a subtle address and impassible humor such as I have not met with even in the most famous talkers of humanity. He explained the absurdity of the different philosophies which have up to the present time had possession of the human brain, and he even deigned to divulge certain fundamental principles whose possession and benefits I do not find it expedient to share with a single soul. He did not complain of the bad reputation he enjoys in every corner of the world, and assured me that no one was more interested in the suppression of *superstition* than himself, and admitted that the only time he had ever trembled for his power was the day when a preacher had exclaimed from his pulpit: "My beloved brothers, never forget when you hear people boast of our progress in enlightenment, that one of the devil's best ruses is to persuade you that he does not exist!"

[61]

The recollection of this noted orator lead us naturally to the subject of institutions of learning, and my strange table-companion told me that in many cases he did not think it beneath him to inspire the pen, the speech, and the conscience of pedagogues, and that he almost invariably attended in person, although invisible, all academic assemblies.

Encouraged by so much kindness, I asked him for news of God, and whether he had seen him recently. He replied with an indifference tinged with sadness: "We bow to each other when we meet like two well-bred old gentlemen, whose innate courtesy is, nevertheless, not sufficient to wipe out the memory of old grudges."

I doubt if His Highness has ever before accorded such a long interview to a simple mortal, and I feared I must be presuming. At last, as shivering dawn whitened the window panes, this famous character, sung by so many poets and served by so many philosophers who work for his glory without knowing it, said to me: "As I want you to take away an agreeable remembrance of me, I — I, Satan himself — am going to prove to you, in spite of all the ill that is said of me, that I can sometimes be a *good devil,* to use one of your popular expressions. To compensate you for the irremediable loss of your soul, I shall give you the same stake you would have won if chance had been with you, that is the possibility of alleviating and overcoming for your entire life that strange disease of Boredom which is the source of all your ills and all your miserable progress. Never shall you formulate a wish that I will not help you to realize; you shall dominate your vulgar fellowmen; flattery shall be yours, and even adoration; silver, gold, diamonds, and fairy palaces shall come seeking you out, begging to be accepted without your having to lift a finger to obtain them; you shall change nationality and country as often as your fancy dictates; you shall know all the intoxication of pleasure, without satiety, in lovely lands where it is always warm and where the women smell as sweet as the flowers

— et cetera, et cetera . . .," he added as he rose and dismissed me with a kindly smile.

If I had not been afraid of embarrassing him before that vast assembly, I would willingly have fallen on my knees at the feet of this generous gambler, to thank him for his unheard-of munificence. But after I had left him, little by little, doubt crept back into my breast; I no longer dared to believe in such prodigious good fortune, and when I went to bed that night, idiotically saying my prayers out of habit and half asleep, I murmured: "Oh, God! Lord, my God! Make the devil keep his promise!"

XXX

THE ROPE

To Edouard Manet

"Illusions," said my friend, "are as innumerable, perhaps, as the relations of men to each other and of men and things. And when the illusion disappears, when, that is, we see persons or things as they really are, detached from ourselves, we have a strange, complex feeling, half regret for the vanished phantom, half agreeable surprise at the appearance of this novel, of this real thing. If there is one obvious, ordinary, never-changing phenomenon of a nature to make misapprehension impossible, it is surely mother-love. It is as difficult to imagine a mother without mother-love as light without heat; is it not then perfectly legitimate to attribute all a mother's acts and words, in regard to her child, to mother-love? And yet, let me tell you this little story in which you will see how I was singularly deceived by this most natural illusion.

"By my profession as a painter I am impelled to scrutinize attentively every face, every physiognomy that comes my way, and you know what delight we painters take in that faculty which gives more zest and significance to life for us than for other men. In the out of the way neighborhood where I live, and where great grassy spaces still separate the houses, I used to watch a certain little boy whose eager, mischievous face appealed to me more than any of the others. He posed for me several times, and I would disguise him, sometimes as a little gypsy, sometimes as an angel, sometimes as the mythological Cupid. I painted him with the vagrant musician's violin, with the Crown of Thorns and the Nails of the Cross, and with the torch of Eros. Finally I came to take such delight in the young-ster's drollery that one day I asked his parents, who were very poor, to let me keep him, promising to dress him well, to give him a little money, and not to impose on him any tasks more onerous than cleaning my brushes and running my errands. After he had been well scrubbed, the boy was really charming, and the life he lead with me seemed to him paradise compared to that in his parent's wretched hole. Only I must say the little fellow often astonished me by strange fits of precocious melancholy, as well as by an immoderate craving, soon mani-festing itself, for sugar and spirits; it had come to such a pass that one day when I had noticed that, in spite of my many warnings, he had been pilfering again, I threatened to send him back to his parents. I then went out and my affairs kept me away for a considerable time.

"What was my horror and stupefaction when, opening my door, the first object that met my eyes was my little man, the mischievous little companion of my life, hanging from that wardrobe over there! His feet almost touched the ground; a chair, which he had evidently kicked out of the way, was over-turned beside him; his head was convulsively twisted to one side; his face swollen, and his eyes, wide open, stared with a terrifying fixity that gave the illusion of life. To take him down was not as easy a task as you might think. He was already stiff, and I felt an inexplicable revulsion to letting him drop to the floor. I was obliged to sustain his whole weight with one arm while, with my free hand, I cut the rope. But that was not all; the little wretch had used such a thin rope that it had sunk deep into the flesh, and to free his neck I had to dig for the rope between the swellings with a pair of fine scissors.

"I neglected to tell you that I had, in the first place, called lustily for help; but my neighbors had refused to come to my assistance, true in this to the prejudice of civilized man who, I do not know why, will have no part in the affairs of the hanged. Finally a doctor arrived who declared that the child had been dead for several hours already. When later we had to undress him for burial, the body was so rigid that, unable to bend his limbs, we were forced to cut his clothes to remove them.

"The police sergeant, to whom naturally I had to report the suicide, eyed me narrowly, saying: 'Something suspicious looking about this,' prompted, no doubt, both by personal bias and the professional habit of trying to strike terror into innocent and guilty alike.

"The supreme task was still to be accomplished, the very thought of which caused me an unbearable anguish: his parents had to be told. My feet simply refused to take me. At last I summoned up all my courage. But to my great astonishment the mother remained unmoved, not a tear trickled from her eyes. I attributed this to the extreme horror she must feel, and I recalled the well-known saying: 'The deepest sorrows are silent.' As for the father, half churlish, half pensive, all he found to say was: 'Well, it's all for the best, I guess. He would have come to a bad end anyway!'

"Meanwhile the body was laid out on my sofa, and I was taking care of the final details assisted by a servant, when the mother entered my studio. She wanted to see the body of her son, she said. I could hardly prevent her revelling in her sorrow or refuse her this supreme and somber consolation. Then she asked me to show her the place where her boy had hanged himself. 'Oh! No, Madam,' I replied, 'that will be too painful for you.' And, as involuntarily my eyes turned toward the fatal wardrobe, I saw with repugnance, mixed with horror, that the nail had been left in the panel with a long piece of rope still dangling from it. I rushed over to remove these last vestiges of the tragedy, and was about to fling them out of the open window, when the poor woman seized my arm and in an irresistible voice said: 'Oh! Monsieur, let me have them! I beg, I implore you!' Her despair I decided must have so crazed her that she had been seized with a passionate longing for the instrument of her son's death, and desired to keep it as a horrible and cherished relic. She took possession of the rope and the nail.

[66]

"At last! At last! It was over. There was nothing more for me to do but to go back to work, and more furiously than ever, trying to drive out the little corpse that filled every convolution of my brain, and whose ghost haunted me with his great staring eyes. But the following day I received a pile of letters: some from tenants in my own building, some from neighboring houses; one from the first floor; another from the second; another from the third and so forth and so on; some in a half playful style, some jokingly trying to hide the eagerness in their request; the others grossly brazen and misspelled, but all with the same object in view: to persuade me to let them have a piece of the fatal and beatific rope. Among the signatures, I must say, there were more women's than men's; but, I assure you, they did not all come from the lower classes by any means. I have kept those letters.

"It was then, suddenly, that it dawned upon me why the mother had been so anxious to get possession of the rope, and the sort of trade she was contemplating for consolation."

XXXI

VOCATIONS

IN A LOVELY garden where the autumnal sun seemed to linger with pleasure, under a sky, already noticeably tinged with green, in which the golden clouds sailed like cruising continents, four beautiful children, four boys, tired probably of their games, were talking.

One of them said: "Yesterday I was taken to the theatre. There are great sad palaces, and behind them you can see the sky and the sea; there are men and women, very serious and sad too, and much more beautiful and beautifully dressed than any you have ever seen, who speak to each other in sing-song voices. They threaten each other, they implore, they are in despair, and they are always putting their hands to daggers thrust into their belts. Oh! but it is beautiful! The women are much more beautiful and much taller than any that come to our house, and although they are terrifying with their great hollow eyes and their flaming red cheeks, you can't help falling in love with them. You're frightened and you want to cry, but somehow you are happy too. . . . And then, what's funnier still, it makes you want to be dressed like that too, to say and do the same things, and to speak in the same kind of voice . . ."

One of the four children, who for some time had not been listening to his comrade's discourse, and had been looking with extraordinary fixity at some distant point in the sky, suddenly exclaimed: "Look, look up there! Do you see *him?* He is sitting on that little cloud all by itself that is the color of fire and moves so slowly. I think *He* is looking at us too."

"But who are you talking about?" asked the others.

"God!" he replied in a tone of complete conviction. "Ah!

He is far away already; soon we shan't be able to see him any more. I suppose he is going to visit other countries. See, he is about to disappear behind that row of trees on the horizon ... and now he is going down behind the church tower ... Ah! you can't see him any more!" And for a long while the child remained staring in the same direction at the line that separates heaven and earth, his eyes bright with an indescribable expression of ecstasy and regret.

"How silly he is with his old God that nobody sees but him!" said a third, a boy whose whole little being was bursting with animation and an extraordinary vitality. "Now, I can tell you something that happened to me a bit more interesting than your theatres and your clouds. A few days ago my parents took me with them on a trip, and as the inn where we stopped was crowded and there were no more beds, they decided that I should sleep in the same bed as my nurse." He drew his comrades closer around him and lowered his voice. "It certainly gives you a funny feeling not to be sleeping alone, and to be in bed with your nurse, and in the dark. I couldn't sleep so, while she was sleeping, I amused myself stroking her arms and her neck and her shoulders. Her arms and neck are much bigger than all other women's, and her skin is so soft, so awfully soft, it feels like writing paper or tissue paper. I enjoyed it so much I would have gone on forever, only I was afraid, afraid first of all of waking her, and afraid too of I don't know what. So then I buried my head in her hair, as thick as a horse's mane covering her back, and I tell you it smelt as good as the flowers in this garden smell now. If you ever get the chance try to do the same — you'll see!"

While talking, the eyes of the young author of this revelation had widened with a sort of stupefaction at what he was still feeling, and the light of the setting sun playing in his untidy red curls seemed to be lighting up a sulphurous aureole of passion. It was easy enough to foresee that this boy would not waste his life looking for God in the clouds, and that he would frequently find him somewhere else.

Finally, the fourth boy said: "You know that it isn't awfully amusing for me at home. I am never taken to the theatre — my guardian is much too stingy; God never pays any attention to me and my boredom, and I haven't any beautiful nurse to cuddle. I have often thought that what I'd like most to do would be to walk straight ahead of me without knowing where I was going and without any one bothering about me, and always seeing new countries. I am never content anywhere, and wherever I am, I always think it would be better somewhere else. Well, at the last fair we went to in the next village, I saw three men who live the way I'd like to live. You fellows didn't notice them. They were tall, they were almost black, and haughty, although dressed in rags, with an air of asking favors of nobody. Their enormous black eyes shone terribly when they were playing their music; such astonishing music; first it made you want to dance, then it made you want to cry, or both at once, and it would drive you mad if you listened to it too long. One of them, as he drew his bow across the strings of his violin, seemed to be telling of some sorrow, the other, making his little hammers jump about on the strings of the tiny piano hung from a strap around his neck, seemed to be making fun of his partners' lamentations, while the third, every now and then, would bring his cymbals together with a violent crash. They were enjoying themselves so much that they went on playing their wild music even after the crowd had dispersed. Finally they picked up their pennies, put their baggage on their backs and went away. But I wanted to find out where they lived so I followed them at a distance to where the forest begins, and then I understood — they don't live any where.

" 'Shall we put up the tent'? one of them asked.

" 'What's the use on a beautiful night like this!' another replied.

"The third who was counting their earnings, said: 'These people have no feeling for music and their wives dance like bears. Luckily we'll be in Austria in a month where people are more agreeable.'

[70]

" 'We'd do better to go toward Spain,' said one of the others, 'the season's pretty well along. I'm all for avoiding the rains and wetting nothing but our whistles.'

"You see, I've remembered everything. After that each of them drank a cup of brandy and went to sleep, their faces turned toward the stars. At first I wanted to beg them to take me with them, and to teach me to play their instruments; but I didn't dare, probably because it is always so hard to decide anything at all, and also because I was afraid of being caught before I could get out of France."

From the indifferent air of his three companions I decided that this youngster was already one of the *un-understood*. I looked at him curiously; there was in his eye and in his forehead that something so prematurely fatal which invariably alienates sympathy, but which for some reason excited mine, and to such an extent that for an instant I had the strange idea that I might, unknown to me, have a brother.

The sun had gone down. Night in all its solemnity had taken its place. The boys separated, each setting out, all unconsciously and as luck and circumstances would decide, to cultivate his fortune, to scandalize his neighbors, and to gravitate toward glory or dishonor.

XXXII

THE THYRSUS

To Franz Liszt.

WHAT IS a thyrsus? In its religious and poetic sense it is the sacerdotal emblem of priests and priestesses when celebrating the deity whose interpreters they are. But physically it is just a stick, a simple stick, a staff to hold up hops, a prop for training vines, straight, hard and dry. Around this stick in capricious convolutions, stems and flowers play and gambol, some sinuous and wayward, others hanging like bells, or like goblets up-side-down. And an amazing resplendence surges from this complexity of lines and of delicate or brilliant colors. Does it not seem as though the curvilinear and the spiral lines were courting the straight line, and were dancing around it in mute admiration? Does it not seem as though all those delicate corollas, all those calyxes, in an explosion of scents and colors, were executing a mysterious fandango around the hieratic rod? But what imprudent mortal would dare to say whether the flowers and the vines have been made for the stick, or whether the stick is not a pretext for displaying the beauty of the vines and the flowers? The thyrsus is an image of your astonishing quality, great and venerated Master, dear Bacchante of mysterious and passionate Beauty. Never did a nymph, driven to frenzy by the invincible Bacchus, shake her thyrsus over the heads of her maddened companions with such energy and wantonness as you your genius over the hearts of your brothers. The rod is your will, steady, straight, and firm, and the flowers, the wanderings of your fancy around your will, the feminine element executing its bewitching pirouettes around the male.

Straight line and arabesque, intention and expression, inflexibility of the will, sinuosity of the word, unity of the goal, variety of the means, all-powerful and indivisible amalgam of genius, what analyst would have the detestable courage to divide and separate you?

Dear Liszt, through the mists and beyond the rivers, in distant cities where pianos sing your glory, and where printing presses translate your wisdom, wherever you may be, whether surrounded by the splendors of the eternal city, or in the mists of those dreamy countries Gambrinus consoles, improvising songs of joy and of ineffable sorrow, or confiding to paper your abstruse meditations, singer of Pleasure and of eternal Anguish, philosopher, poet, artist, I salute you in immortality!

GET DRUNK

ONE SHOULD always be drunk. That's the great thing; the only question. Not to feel the horrible burden of Time weighing on your shoulders and bowing you to the earth, you should be drunk without respite.

Drunk with what? With wine, with poetry, or with virtue, as you please. But get drunk.

And if sometimes you should happen to awake, on the stairs of a palace, on the green grass of a ditch, in the dreary solitude of your own room, and find that your drunkenness is ebbing or has vanished, ask the wind and the wave, ask star, bird, or clock, ask everything that flies, everything that moans, everything that flows, everything that sings, everything that speaks, ask them the time; and the wind, the wave, the star, the bird and the clock will all reply: "It is Time to get drunk! If you are not to be the martyred slaves of Time, be perpetually drunk! With wine, with poetry, or with virtue, as you please."

ALREADY!

A HUNDRED TIMES already the sun had sprung, radiant or sad, out of the immense vat of the sea, a hundred times had plunged back, sparkling or surly, into the vast bath of evening. For a number of days we had been able to contemplate the other side of the firmament, and to decipher the celestial alphabet of the antipodes. And the passengers grumbled and growled. The approach of land seemed even to aggravate their torments. "Are we never again to enjoy sleep without being tossed about by the waves and kept awake by the wind that snores louder than we do? Are we never again to eat meat that is not as salty as the element beneath us? Or sit quietly in an immovable armchair to digest it?"

Some thought of their firesides, were homesick for their unfaithful, ill-tempered wives and noisy offspring. All were so obsessed by the image of the absent land that they would, I really believe, have eaten grass as eagerly as herbiverous animals.

At last we came in sight of the coast; and as we drew nearer we could see that it was a magnificent and dazzling land. All life's sweet sounds seemed to come from it in a soft murmur, and the shores, rich in vegetation of every kind, exhaled for miles around a delicious fragrance of fruits and flowers.

Immediately everybody was happy, everybody abdicated his bad humor. All quarrels were forgotten, all wrongs reciprocally pardoned; preconcerted duels were erased from the memory, and rancors vanished like smoke.

I alone was sad, inconceivably sad. Like a priest whose God has been snatched from him, I could not without heartbreaking bitterness tear myself away from the sea, so monotonously seductive, so infinitely varied in her terrible simplicity and seeming to contain and to represent by all her changing moods, the angers, smiles, humors, agonies and ecstasies of all the souls who have lived, who live, or who will some day live!

In saying farewell to this incomparable beauty, I was sad unto death; and that is why when all my companions were saying, "At last!" I could only cry, *"Already!"*

Nevertheless, there it was, land with its noises, its passions, all its wares and its festivities; it was a dazzling, a magnificent land full of promises, and from which a mysterious perfume of musk and roses came drifting out to us, and, like an amorous whisper, the myriad music of life.

W I N D O W S

LOOKING from outside into an open window one never sees as much as when one looks through a closed window. There is nothing more profound, more mysterious, more pregnant, more insidious, more dazzling than a window lighted by a single candle. What one can see out in the sunlight is always less interesting than what goes on behind a window pane. In that black or luminous square life lives, life dreams, life suffers.

Across the ocean of roofs I can see a middle-aged woman, her face already lined, who is forever bending over something and who never goes out. Out of her face, her dress and her gestures, out of practically nothing at all, I have made up this woman's story, or rather legend, and sometimes I tell it to myself and weep.

If it had been an old man I could have made up his just as well.

And I go to bed proud to have lived and to have suffered in some one besides myself.

Perhaps you will say "Are you sure that your story is the real one?" But what does it matter what reality is outside myself, so long as it has helped me to live, to feel that I am, and what I am?

THE DESIRE TO PAINT

UNHAPPY perhaps is man, but happy the artist torn by desire!

I am consumed by a desire to paint the woman who appeared to me so rarely and who so quickly fled, like a beautiful regretted thing the voyager leaves behind as he is carried away into the night. How long it is now, since she disappeared!

She is beautiful and more than beautiful; she is surprising. Darkness in her abounds, and all that she inspires is nocturnal and profound. Her eyes are two caverns where mystery dimly glistens, and like a lightning flash, her glance illuminates: it is an explosion in the dark.

I have compared her to a black sun, if one can imagine a black star pouring out light and happiness. But she makes one think rather of the moon, which has surely marked her with its portentous influence; not the white moon of idylls which resembles a frigid bride, but the sinister and intoxicating moon that hangs deep in a stormy night, hurtled by the driven clouds; not the discreet and peaceful moon that visits pure men while they sleep, but the moon torn from the sky, the conquered and indignant moon that the Thessalian Witches cruelly compel to dance on the frightened grass!

That little forehead is inhabited by a tenacious will and a desire for prey. Yet, in the lower part of this disturbing countenance, with sensitive nostrils quivering for the unknown and the impossible, bursts, with inexpressible loveliness, a wide mouth, red and white and alluring, that makes one dream of the miracle of a superb flower blooming on volcanic soil.

There are women who inspire you with the desire to conquer them and to take your pleasure of them; but this one fills you only with the desire to die slowly beneath her gaze.

THE MOON'S FAVORS

THE MOON, who is caprice itself, looked in through your window as you lay asleep in your cradle, and said: "This child pleases me."

And downily descending her stairway of cloud, she passed through the window pane without a sound. Then she stretched herself over you with a mother's careful tenderness, and left her colors on your face. That is why your eyes are green and your cheeks extraordinarily pale. And it was when you looked at this visitor that your eyes grew so wondrously large; and she clasped your throat so tenderly that you have wanted to weep ever since.

At the same time, in the fullness of her joy, the Moon pervaded the whole room like a phosphoric atmosphere, like a luminous poison; and all that living radiance thought and said: "By my kiss I make you eternally mine. You shall be beautiful as I am beautiful. You shall love what I love and what loves me: water, clouds, silence and the night; the green unfathomable sea; water without form and multiform; the place where you are not; the lover you will never know; monstrous flowers; delirious perfume; languorous cats who lie on pianos and moan like women with sweet and husky voices!

"And you shall be loved by my lovers, courted by my courtiers. You shall be the queen of all men with green eyes, whose throats I have clasped in my nocturnal caresses; of those who love the sea, the green, unfathomable, tumultuous sea; water without form and multi-form; the place where they are not, the woman they will never know, sinister flowers like the censers of a strange religion, perfumes that trouble the will,

[79]

savage and voluptuous beasts that are the emblems of their madness."

And that is why, dear, spoilt, accursed child, I am lying at your feet searching you all over for the reflection of the dread Goddess, the fateful godmother and poison-nurse of all *moon-mad men.*

WHICH IS THE REAL ONE?

I ONCE KNEW a certain Bénédicta who filled earth and air with the ideal, and whose eyes scattered the seeds of longing for greatness, beauty and glory, for everything that makes a man believe in immortality.

But this miraculous girl was too beautiful to live long; and so it was that, only a few days after I had come to know her, she died, and I buried her with my own hands one day when Spring was swaying its censer over the graveyards. I buried her with my own hands and shut her into a coffin of scented and incorruptible wood like the coffers of India.

And while my eyes still gazed on the spot where my treasure lay buried, all at once I saw a little creature who looked singularly like the deceased, stamping up and down on the fresh earth in a strange hysterical frenzy, and who said as she shrieked with laughter: "Look at me! I am the real Bénédicta! a perfect hussy! And to punish you for your blindness and your folly, you shall love me as I am."

But I was furious and cried: "No! no! no!" And to emphasize my refusal I stamped so violently on the earth that my leg sank into the new dug grave up to my knee; and now, like a wolf caught in a trap, I am held fast, perhaps forever, to the grave of the ideal.

A THOROUGH-BRED

SHE IS very ugly. She is nevertheless delectable. Time and Love have marked her with their claws, and cruelly taught her that every instant, every kiss, steal something of youth and freshness.

She is really ugly. She is, if you like, ant, spider, skeleton even; but she is also the draught that refreshes, magic and magistery! In short she is exquisite.

Time could not spoil the sparkling harmony of her walk, nor alter the indestructible elegance of her panoply. Love has not tainted the sweetness of her child's breath; nor has Time torn out a hair of her abounding mane, from whose wild perfumes all the mad vitality of the French Midi is exhaled Nimes, Aix, Arles, Avignon, Narbonne, Toulouse — amorous, charming cities, blessed by the sun!

Vainly have time and love sunk their teeth into her; they have not in the least diminished the illusive but eternal charm of her boyish breast.

Worn, perhaps, but not weary, and always gallant, she makes one think of one of those thorough-breds that the eye of a true connoisseur will always recognize even when harnessed to a hired hack or lumbering coach.

And then she is so gentle and so fervent! She loves as one loves in the fall of the year; the coming of winter, it would seem, has lighted a fresh fire in her heart, and there is never anything tiresome about the servility of her tenderness.

THE MIRROR

AN APPALLING-looking man enters and looks at himself in a mirror.

"Why do you look at yourself in the glass, since the sight of your reflection can only be painful to you?"

The appalling-looking man replies: "Sir, according to the immortal principles of '89, all men are equal before the law; therefore I have the right to look at myself in the glass; with pleasure or pain, that is an entirely personal matter."

In respect of common sense, I was certainly right; but from the point of view of the law, he was not wrong.

SEA-PORTS

A SEA-PORT is a pleasant place for a soul worn out with life's struggles. The wide expanse of sky, the mobile clouds, the ever changing colors of the sea, the flashing beams of the light-houses form a prism marvelously designed to gladden, without ever tiring the eye. The ships with their long slim lines and complicated rigging that so gracefully ride the swells, serve to keep alive in the soul a taste for rhythm and beauty. And, above all, for the man who has lost all curiosity, all ambition, there is a sort of mysterious and aristocratic pleasure in watching, as he reclines in the belvedere or leans on the mole, all the bustle of people leaving, of people returning, people who still have enough energy to have desires, who still desire to voyage, who still desire to get rich.

PORTRAITS OF SOME MISTRESSES

IN A MAN's boudoir, that is, in the smoking-room of an elegant gambling-house, four men were smoking and drinking. They were not precisely young, nor yet old, they were neither handsome nor ugly; but young or old, they all bore the unmistakable signs of veterans of pleasure, that indescribable something, that cold ironic sadness which says plainly: "We have lived to the full, and we are looking for something we can love and respect."

One of them turned the conversation to the subject of women. It would have been more philosophical not to talk about them at all; but after drinking, intelligent men are not above commonplace discourse. And one listens to what is said as one listens to dance music.

"Every man," he began, "was once Cherubin's age. That is the time when, if there are no dryads about, one embraces the trees. It is the first degree of love. In the second degree one begins to choose. To be able to discriminate is already a sign of decadence. It is then that one decidedly looks for beauty. As for me, gentlemen, I am proud to say that I have long ago arrived at the climacteric period of the third degree when beauty itself no longer suffices unless it be seasoned with perfumes, jewels, et cetera. I admit that I sometimes long for the fourth degree as for an unknown happiness, since it must, I am sure, be distinguished by absolute calm. But throughout my life, except at the age of Cherubin, I have always been more affected than other men by the enervating stupidity, the irritating mediocrity of women. What I like about animals is their simplicity. You may judge then how my last mistress made me suffer.

"She was the illegitimate daughter of a prince. Beautiful, that goes without saying; otherwise why should I have taken her? But she spoiled that splendid quality by being indecently, monstrously ambitious. She was the sort of woman who was always wanting to play the man. 'You are not a man! Ah! if I were only a man! Of the two of us, I am really the man!' Such were the insufferable refrains that came out of a mouth from which I wanted only songs to soar. If I let my admiration for a book, a poem, an opera escape me, she would straightway say: 'You think it very forceful, don't you? But are you any judge of forcefulness?' And she would begin to argue.

"One fine day she took up chemistry, and after that I always found a glass mask between her lips and mine. And then, what a prude! If, on occasion, I shocked her by a somewhat too amorous gesture, she would recoil like a sensitive plant."

"But how did it end?" interrupted one of the men. "I never knew you had so much patience."

"God," he replied, "invariably supplies a remedy for every ill. One day I found my Minerva, who had such a thirst for ideal force, *tête-à-tête* with my valet, and in a posture which, I felt, made it incumbent upon me to retire discreetly so as not to make them blush. That evening I dismissed them both, after paying them their wages in arrears."

"Well, as far as I am concerned," went on the man who had interrupted, "I have no one to blame but myself. Happiness entered my house and I failed to recognize her. Not so many years ago, Fate granted me the possession of a woman who was without doubt the sweetest, the most submissive, and the most devoted creature in the world, and who was always ready! And without enthusiasm! 'Of course I want to, since it gives you pleasure.' That was her invariable answer; and, I assure you, if you were to give this wall or that sofa a good bastinado, you would draw from them more sighs than the most furious throes of love ever drew from my mistress's breast. After living

[86]

together for a year she finally confessed that she had never felt the least pleasure in love. The unequal duel ended by disgusting me, and so this incomparable girl got herself married. Some years later the fancy struck me to see her again. After showing me her six beautiful children she said:

" 'Well, dear friend, the wife is still as *virginal* as your mistress was.' Nothing about her had changed. Sometimes I have my regrets. I should have married her."

The others laughed, and the third began in his turn:

"Gentlemen, I have known a sort of pleasure which you have probably neglected. I refer to comedy in love, and comedy that in no way excludes admiration. I admired my last mistress, I believe, more than you loved or hated yours. And every one, like myself, was in admiration before her. Whenever we went to a restaurant, after a few moments, everyone forgot their own food to watch her eat. Even the waiters and the lady presiding over the desk, caught by this contagious ecstasy, forgot their duties. In short, I lived intimately for some time with a living phenomenon. She ate, chewed, munched, devoured, gulped and swallowed with the gayest, most carefree air in the world. She kept me in ecstasy for a long time. She had such a gentle, dreamy, English and romantic way of saying, 'I am hungry.' And day and night, displaying the prettiest teeth imaginable, she would repeat these words which so touched and tickled me at the same time. I could have made a fortune displaying her at street fairs as a *polyphagous monster*. I fed her well but, in spite of that, she left me . . ." — "For a wholesale grocer, no doubt?" — "Well, something of the sort, a kind of commissary clerk who, by some juggler's trick known only to himself, is able to keep the poor child supplied with the rations of several soldiers. That, at least, is what I have always supposed."

"As for me," the fourth one said, "I have endured the most atrocious suffering through the exact opposite of what is known and reproved as feminine selfishness. I find it quite thankless of you, far too fortunate mortals, to complain of the imperfections of your mistresses!"

This was said in all seriousness by a man with a gentle and placid air, and an almost clerical physiognomy, but lighted, unfortunately, by very pale grey eyes; the sort of eyes that say: "I wish it!" or, "You must!" or else, "I never forgive!"

"Nervous as I know you to be, G . . ., cowardly and frivolous as you, K. and J. both are . . . if you had been yoked to a certain woman I have known, you would either have run away, or you would now be dead. I, as you see, survived. Imagine a person incapable of committing the least fault, either of judgment or sentiment; imagine a disposition of a hopeless serenity; a devotion not simulated and without stress; gentleness without weakness, energy without violence. The history of this love affair of mine resembles a voyage, vertiginously monotonous, over a surface as smooth and polished as a mirror that reflected all my feelings, all my gestures, with the ironic fidelity of my own conscience, so that I could never make a thoughtless gesture, never indulge in a foolish emotion without immediately perceiving the silent reproach of my inseparable spectre. Love seemed more like a guardianship. I don't know how many misguided acts she saved me from and that I bitterly regret not having committed! How many debts she made me pay in spite of myself! She deprived me of all the benefits of my personal folly. With a cold impassible ruler she barred all my whims. And, as the final horror, she never asked for gratitude, once the danger was past. How many times I had to keep myself from taking her by the throat and crying: 'Can't you ever be imperfect, miserable woman, so that I can love you without mortification and without anger!' For several years I continued to admire her with hate in my heart. In the end it was not I who died of it!"

"Ah!" said the others, "so she is dead?"

"Yes! It could not go on like that. Love had become a crushing nightmare to me. Do or die, as they say in politics, that was the alternative fate held out for me! One evening, in a woods . . . beside the sea . . . we had taken a melancholy walk during which *her* eyes reflected all the sweetness of heaven, while *my* heart was as hideous as hell . . ."

"What!"

"What do you mean?"

"You mean . . . ?"

"It was inevitable. I have too great a sense of fairness to beat, or to ill-treat, or to dismiss an irreproachable servitor. But I had to find a way of reconciling this sentiment with the horror that the woman inspired in me; that is, I had to get rid of the creature without, however, showing her any disrespect. What would you have had me do with her, *since she was perfect?*"

The three other men looked at him with an uncertain and slightly stupefied expression, half feigning to understand, half implicitly admitting that they felt, as for themselves, incapable of such an inexorable solution, although it had, indeed, been admirably explained.

Then, to kill Time which has such a hardy life, as well as to accelerate Life which flows so slowly, they ordered a few more bottles of wine.

THE GALLANT MARKSMAN

As THE CARRIAGE was going through the woods, he had it stop
near a shooting gallery, saying that it would be pleasant to
take a shot or two to kill Time. And is not killing that monster
the most ordinary and legitimate occupation of all of us?
Gallantly, then, he held out his hand to his dear, delectable,
and execrable wife, to the mysterious woman to whom he owed
so many pleasures and so many pains, and perhaps a large
part of his genius as well.

Several shots went wide of the mark; one even buried
itself in the ceiling; and as the charming creature began to
laugh hilariously, twitting her husband on his want of dexterity,
he turned toward her brusquely and said: "You see that doll
over there to the right, with its nose in the air and its haughty
mien? Well now, my dear angel, *I am going to imagine it is
you.*" And he closed his eyes and fired. The doll was neatly
decapitated.

Then bowing to his dear, delectable and execrable wife,
his inevitable and pitiless Muse, and respectfully kissing her
hand, he added: "Ah, dear angel, thank you so much for my
dexterity!"

THE SOUP AND THE CLOUDS

MY DEAR little mad beloved was serving my dinner, and I was looking out of the open dining-room window contemplating those moving architectural marvels that God constructs out of mist, edifices of the impalpable. And as I looked I was saying to myself: "All those phantasmagoria are almost as beautiful as my beloved's beautiful eyes, as the green eyes of my mad monstrous little beloved."

All of a sudden I felt a terrible blow of a fist on my back, and heard a husky and charming voice, an hysterical voice, a hoarse brandy voice, the voice of my dear little beloved, saying: "Aren't you ever going to eat your soup, you damned bastard of a cloud-monger?"

THE SHOOTING GALLERY
AND THE CEMETERY

CEMETERY VIEW TAVERN — "Singular sign," remarked our
foot-traveler, "but well calculated to make any one thirsty!
Certainly the host of this tavern must appreciate Horace and
the poet-pupils of Epicurus. He may even know the supreme
refinement of the Egyptians for whom no feast was complete
without a skeleton, or without some emblem of life's brevity."

And he entered, drank a glass of beer facing the graves,
and slowly smoked a cigar. Then he took a notion to go down
to the cemetery where the grass was so tall and so inviting,
and where such a generous sun held sway.

And certainly heat and sun were rampant there, indeed it
looked as though the drunken sun was sprawled full length on
the carpet of magnificent flowers, manured by dissolution.
The air was full of buzzing life — the life of the infinitely small
— interrupted at regular intervals by shots from a nearby
shooting gallery that burst like the explosion of champagne
corks in the midst of the murmurs of a muted symphony.

Then, his brain heated by the sun, with the hot perfumes of
Death all around him, he heard a voice whispering within the
grave on which he was seated. And the voice said: "A curse
on your targets and on your rifles, turbulent live men who have
so little regard for the dead and their sacred repose. A curse
on your ambitions, a curse on your schemes, impatient mortals
who come to study the art of killing next to Death's sanctuary!
If you only knew how easy it is to win the prize, how easy it
is to hit the mark, and how everything is nothing, except Death,
you would not tire yourselves so, laborious men, and you would

not come here so often to trouble the slumbers of those who
have hit the Mark long ago, the only mark worth hitting, life,
detestable life!"

LOSS OF A HALO

"WHAT! You here, old man? You in such a place! You the
ambrosia eater, the drinker of quintessences! This is really
a surprise."

"My friend, you know my terror of horses and vehicles.
Well, just now as I was crossing the boulevard in a great
hurry, splashing through the mud in the midst of a seething
chaos, and with death galloping at me from every side, I gave
a sudden start and my halo slipped off my head and fell into
the mire of the macadam. I was far too frightened to pick it
up. I decided it was less unpleasant to lose my insignia than
to get my bones broken. Then too, I reflected, every cloud has
a silver lining. I can now go about incognito, be as low as I
please and indulge in debauch like ordinary mortals. So here
I am as you see, exactly like yourself."

"But aren't you going to advertise for your halo, at least?
Or notify the police?"

"No, I think not. I like it here. You are the only person
who has recognized me. Besides I am bored with dignity, and
what's more, it is perfectly delightful to think of some bad poet
picking it up and brazenly putting it on. To make some one
happy, ah, what a pleasure! Especially some one you can
laugh at. Think of X! Think of Z! Don't you see how amusing
it will be?"

MISS BISTOURY

As I was nearing the end of the suburb, walking along under the gas lamps, I felt an arm being slipped into mine, and I heard a voice in my ear, saying: "Aren't you a doctor?"

I looked; it was a tall, robust young woman with very wide-open eyes, hardly any make-up, and long hair flying in the breeze with the strings of her bonnet.

"No, I am not a doctor," I said, "so, kindly let me go." "Oh! Yes! you are a doctor. I can see that. Come home with me. You'll not be sorry, I promise you!" "Yes, yes, I'll come, but later, *after the doctor,* what the devil!" "Ah! Ah!" she said still clinging to my arm and bursting out laughing. "You're a doctor who likes to have his little joke. I've known many like that. Come."

I am passionately fond of mystery because I always hope to discover the solution. So I let myself be piloted by this chance companion, or rather by this unhoped-for enigma.

I omit the description of her wretched lodgings; it can be found in several of the well-known classic French poets. One detail, however, Régnier overlooked: two or three pictures of famous doctors were hanging on the walls.

How I was pampered. A big fire, spiced wine, cigars; and as she offered me these good things, and herself lighted my cigar, this fantastic creature said: "Now make yourself comfortable, my dear, make yourself at home. It will bring back those good days of your youth at the hospital. But what's this? Where ever did you get these gray hairs? You weren't like that not so long ago when you were L . . . 's intern. I remember you were always his assistant for serious operations. That was a man who liked to cut and hack and carve, I tell you! It was always you who handed him the instruments, the thread and the sponges. And how proudly he used to say, looking at his watch after the operation: 'Five minutes, gentlemen!' Oh! I go everywhere. I certainly know doctors."

A few minutes later she went on with the same tune, saying: "You are a doctor, aren't you, my lamb?"

This unintelligible refrain made me leap to my feet. "No!" I cried furiously.

"Surgeon then?"

"No! No! unless it would be to cut off your head. Blessed-holy-ciborium-of-a-holy-mackerel!"

"Wait," she went on, "let me show you."

And from her wardrobe she took out a bundle of papers that contained nothing more nor less than pictures of famous doctors of the day, lithographs by Maurin which for years might have been seen on the Quai Voltaire.

"Look, do you know this one?"

"Yes, it's X. Besides his name is at the bottom. But I happen to know him personally."

"Why, of course you do, I knew that. Look, that is Z., the one who used to say when speaking of X.: 'That monster who wears the blackness of his soul on his face!' And simply because they weren't in agreement on a certain matter. How we used to laugh about it in Medical. Do you remember? — See, that's K., the one who informed against the insurgents who were his patients in the hospital. It was at the time of the uprisings. How could such a handsome man have such a hard heart? — Now that is W., the famous English doctor; I caught him when he came to Paris. He looks like a young lady, doesn't he?"

And as I was fingering another bundle tied with string also lying on the table: "Wait," she said, "those are the interns, and this bundle is the externs."

And she spread fan-like a mass of photographs of very much younger faces.

[96]

"When we meet next time you'll give me your photograph too, won't you darling?"

"But," I said, also pursuing my *idée fixe*, "why do you think I am a doctor?"

"It's because you're so sweet and so good to women."

"Singular logic," I thought.

"Oh! I never make a mistake; I have known so many. I love them so, all these gentlemen, that although I am not sick I go to see them sometimes for nothing, just to see them. There are some who say to me coldly: 'You are not sick at all!' But there are others who understand me because I am nice to them."

"And when they don't understand you . . . ?"

"Well! as I have bothered them *for nothing*, I leave ten francs on the mantlepiece. They are so good, so gentle, doctors! I have discovered at the *Pitié* a young intern who is as pretty as an angel, and who is so polite! And who has to work, poor boy! His comrades told me he didn't have a penny because his parents are so poor they can't send him anything. That gave me courage. After all, I am not bad looking although not too young. I said to him: 'Come to see me, come to see me often. With me you don't have to worry; I don't need money.' But, of course, I made him understand in all sorts of ways, I didn't just tell him brutally like that; I was so afraid of humiliating him, the dear boy! Well, you know, I've got a funny notion, and I don't dare tell him. I'd like him to come to see me with his instrument case and his apron, and even with a little blood on it."

She said this with perfect simplicity, as a man might say to an actress he was in love with: "I should like you to be dressed in the costume you wear in the famous role you created."

And I still obstinately persisted: "Can you remember the time and the occasion when you first felt this particular passion?"

I had some difficulty in making her understand. Finally

I succeeded. But then she replied with such a sad air, and, as I remember, with downcast eyes: "I don't know ... I don't remember."

What oddities one finds in big cities when one knows how to roam and how to look! Life swarms with innocent monsters. Lord, my God, You the Creator, you the Master; you who have made both Law and Liberty; you the sovereign who permits, you the judge who pardons; you who contain all motives and all causes, and who, perhaps, have put a taste for the horrible in my mind in order to convert my heart, like the cure at the point of the knife; Lord have pity on, have pity on mad men and mad women! O Creator! can monsters exist in the eyes of the One who alone knows why they exist, who alone knows how they *have been made* and how they could *not have been made*.

XLVIII

ANYWHERE OUT OF THE WORLD

LIFE is a hospital where every patient is obsessed by the desire of changing beds. One would like to suffer opposite the stove, another is sure he would get well beside the window.

It always seems to me that I should be happy anywhere but where I am, and this question of moving is one that I am eternally discussing with my soul.

"Tell me, my soul, poor chilly soul, how would you like to live in Lisbon? It must be warm there, and you would be as blissful as a lizard in the sun. It is a city by the sea; they say that it is built of marble, and that its inhabitants have such a horror of the vegetable kingdom that they tear up all the trees. You see it is a country after my own heart; a country entirely made of mineral and light, and with liquid to reflect them."

My soul does not reply.

"Since you are so fond of being motionless and watching the pageantry of movement, would you like to live in the beatific land of Holland? Perhaps you could enjoy yourself in that country which you have so long admired in paintings on museum walls. What do you say to Rotterdam, you who love forests of masts, and ships that are moored on the doorsteps of houses?"

My soul remains silent.

"Perhaps you would like Batavia better? There, moreover, we should find the wit of Europe wedded to the beauty of the tropics."

Not a word. Can my soul be dead?

"Have you sunk into so deep a stupor that you are happy only in your unhappiness? If that is the case, let us fly to countries that are the counterfeits of Death. I know just the place for us, poor soul. We will pack up our trunks for Torneo. We will go still farther, to the farthest end of the Baltic Sea; still farther from life if possible; we will settle at the Pole. There the sun only obliquely grazes the earth, and the slow alternations of daylight and night abolish variety and increase that other half of nothingness, monotony. There we can take deep baths of darkness, while sometimes for our entertainment, the Aurora Borealis will shoot up its rose-red sheafs like the reflections of the fireworks of hell!"

At last my soul explodes! "Anywhere! Just so it is out of the world!"

XLIX

BEAT UP THE POOR

For FIFTEEN days I had shut myself up in my room and had surrounded myself with the most popular books of the day (that was sixteen or seventeen years ago); I am speaking of books that treat of the art of making people happy, wise, and rich in twenty-four hours. I had digested — or rather swallowed — all the lucubrations of all the purveyors of public happiness — of those who advise the poor to become slaves, and of those who encourage them to believe that they are all dethroned kings. It will be readily understood that I was in a dazed state of mind bordering on idiocy.

Nevertheless I seemed to be conscious of an obscure germ of an idea buried deep in my mind, far superior to the whole catalogue of old wives' remedies I had so recently scanned. But it was still only the idea of an idea, something infinitely vague.

And I left my room with a terrible thirst. The passion for bad literature engenders a proportionate need for fresh air and cooling drinks.

As I was about to enter a bar, a beggar held out his hat to me and looked at me with one of those unforgettable expressions which, if spirit moved matter or if a magnetizer's eye ripened grapes, would overturn thrones.

At the same time I heard a voice whispering in my ear, a voice I recognized perfectly; it was the voice of my good Angel, or good Demon, who accompanies me everywhere. Since Socrates had his good Demon, why should not I have my good Angel, why should not I, like Socrates, have the honor of receiving a certificate of madness signed by the subtle Lelut and the knowing Baillarger?

There is, however, this difference between Socrates' Demon and mine, that his Demon appeared to him only to forbid, to warn or to prevent, whereas mine deigns to advise, suggest, persuade. Poor Socrates had only a censor; mine is a great affirmer, mine is a Demon of action, a Demon of combat.

Well, this is what the voice whispered to me: "A man is the equal of another only if he can prove it, and to be worthy of liberty a man must fight for it."

Immediately I leaped upon the beggar. With a blow of my fist I closed one of his eyes which in an instant grew as big as a ball. I broke one of my finger nails breaking two of his teeth and since, having been born delicate and never having learned to box, I knew I could not knock out the old man quickly, I seized him by the collar with one hand and with the other took him by the throat and began pounding his head against the wall. I must admit that I had first taken the precaution of looking around me and I felt sure that in this deserted suburb no policeman would disturb me for some time.

Then, having by a vigorous kick in the back, strong enough to break his shoulder blades, felled the sexegenarian, I picked up a large branch that happened to be lying on the ground, and beat him with the obstinate energy of a cook tenderizing a beefsteak.

Suddenly — O miracle! O bliss of the philosopher when he sees the truth of his theory verified! — I saw that antique carcass turn over, jump up with a force I should never have expected in a machine so singularly out of order; and with a look of hate that seemed to me a very *good omen,* the decrepit vagabond hurled himself at me and proceeded to give me two black eyes, to knock out four of my teeth and, with the same branch I had used, to beat me to a pulp. Thus it was that my energetic treatment had restored his pride and given him new life.

I then, by many signs, finally made him understand that I considered the argument settled, and getting up I said to him with all the satisfaction of one of the Porch sophists: "Sir, *you are my equal!* I beg you to do me the honor of sharing my purse. And remember, if you are really philanthropic, when any of your colleagues asks you for alms you must apply the theory which I have just had the *painful* experience of trying out on you."

He swore that he had understood my theory, and that he would follow my advice.

THE FAITHFUL DOG

To M. Joseph Stevens.

MY ADMIRATION for Buffon has never made me blush even before the young writers of my generation. But it is not that painter of majestic nature I would call to my aid today. No. Today I should prefer to appeal to Stern, to whom I would say: "Descend from the skies or rise from the Elysian Fields, sentimental jester, incomparable jester, and inspire me with a song worthy of you on behalf of the poor dog, the faithful dog! Return astride that famous ass of yours, which always accompanies you in the memory of posterity; and above all let him not forget to bring along, daintily held between his lips, your immortal macaroon!"

Away, academic muse! I'll have nothing to do with that pedantic old prude. No, I invoke the friendly, lively muse of cities to help me sing the song of the faithful dog, the mangy dog, the pitiful dog, the dog everybody kicks around because he is dirty and covered with fleas, except the poor man whose companion he is, and the poet who looks upon him with a brotherly eye.

But the devil take your pedigreed fop! The vain impertinent quadruped, King-Charles, Dane, pup or lap-dog, always so pleased with himself that he darts around visitors' legs or bounds indiscreetly into their laps. He is as turbulent as a child, as stupid as a prostitute, and often as surly and insolent as a servant! Above all, the devil take those four-legged snakes called greyhounds, that do nothing but shake and haven't enough flair to pick up their own master's scent, not enough sense in those flattened heads to play dominoes.

To their baskets with them! All those tiresome parasites! Back to their silken and tufted baskets! For I sing the mangy dog, the pitiful, the homeless dog, the roving dog, the circus dog, the dog whose instinct, like that of the gypsy and the strolling player, has been so wonderfully sharpened by necessity, marvelous mother and true patroness of native wit.

I sing the luckless dog who wanders alone through the winding ravines of huge cities, or the one who blinks up at some poor outcast of society with his spiritual eyes, as much as to say: "Take me with you, and out of our joint misery we will make a kind of happiness."

"*Where do dogs go?*" Nestor Roqueplan once asked in an immortal article which he has doubtlessly forgotten, and which I alone, and perhaps Sainte-Beuve, still remember today.

Where do dogs go, you ask, unobservant man? They go about their business.

Business appointments, love affairs. Through fog, through snow, through mire, under the canicular sun, in pelting rain, they go, they come, they trot, and skulk in and out of carriage wheels, driven by their fleas, their passions, their needs, or their obligations. Like the rest of us, they rise betimes and go seeking their daily bread, or running after pleasure.

Some of them sleep in tumble-down shacks on the outskirts of the city, but regularly every day they come to town at the same hour to beg for alms at the door of some kitchen of the Palais Royale; others, in bands, trot five miles or more to share the meals that certain old maids prepare for them, poor virgins who offer their unemployed hearts to dumb beasts since stupid men have no use for them.

Others who, like run-away negroes, mad with love, leave their countryside to come frisking around a lovely city bitch who is, I'm afraid, a little negligent as to her appearance, but proud, nevertheless, and grateful.

And they are very punctual without memoranda, note-books or card-cases.

Do you know lazy Belgium? And have you admired, as I

have, those sturdy dogs harnessed to the butcher's cart, the milkman's or the baker's, and who make it plain by their triumphant barking, how happy and proud they are to be the horse's rival?

And here are two dogs that belong to an even more civilized order. Allow me to take you to the room of an itinerant clown who is himself absent for the moment. A painted wooden bed without curtains and with rumpled and bug-stained blankets, two cane chairs, an iron stove, a few dilapidated musical instruments. Oh! the dreary furniture! But look, if you please, at those two intelligent personages, dressed up in such sumptuous and such shabby suits, with troubadours' or soldiers' caps on their heads, who are watching with all a sorcerer's vigilance, a nameless concoction simmering on the lighted stove, a long-handled spoon stuck into it like one of those poles atop a new building, announcing that the masonry work is finished.

It seems only fair, don't you think, that such zealous actors should not start out on the road without first fortifying their stomachs with a good, solid soup? And can't you forgive them their evident greediness, the poor devils, who every day have to face the indifference of the public and the injustice of an impressario who always takes the lion's share for himself and who eats more soup all alone than the four little actors put together?

How often I have stood watching them, smiling and moved by these four-footed philosophers, willing slaves, submissive and devoted, that the republic's dictionary might very well designate *public benefactors,* if the republic were not too busy making men *happy* to waste time giving dogs their *due.*

And how many times have I thought that there must be somewhere (after all why not?), as recompense for so much courage, patience and labor, a special paradise for good dogs, poor dogs, mangy dogs and disconsolate dogs. Doesn't Swedenborg affirm that there is one for the Turks and for the Dutch?

The shepherds of Virgil and Theocritus were wont to receive for their various songs, a good cheese, or a new flute of better make, or a goat with swollen udders. The poet, who has sung the song of the poor dog, received as his recompense a waistcoat of a hue that is both rich and faded, making you think of autumnal suns, the beauty of women past their prime, and Indian summer.

No one present at the tavern of the rue Villa Hermosa will ever forget with what eagerness the painter stripped off his waistcoat and handed it to the poet, for he understood how right and fitting it was to honor the faithful dog in song.

Just so, in former times, one of the magnificent Italian tyrants would have offered the divine Aretino, a gem-studded dagger or a court mantle, in return for a precious sonnet or a curious satiric poem.

And every time the poet dons the painter's waistcoat he is forced to think of faithful dogs, philosophic dogs, and of Indian summers and the beauty of women past their prime.

EPILOGUE

Happy of heart I climbed the hill
To contemplate the town in its enormity,
Brothel and hospital, prison, purgatory, hell,

Monstrosities flowering like a flower.
But you, O Satan, patron of my pain,
Know I went not to weep for them in vain.

But like old lecher to old mistress goes,
Seeking but rapture, I sought out this trull
Immense, whose hellish charm resuscitates.

Whether in morning sheets you lie asleep,
Hidden and heavy with a cold, or flaunt
Through night in golden spangled veils,

Infamous City, I adore you! Courtesans
And bandits, you offer me such joys,
The common herd can never understand.

POEMS FROM "FLOWERS OF EVIL"

The themes of some of the prose poems of *Paris Spleen* are similar to those of verse poems in the *Fleurs du Mal* which Baudelaire had written earlier. Five of these poems, in which the "correspondence" is most apparent, have been chosen for comparison.

HER HAIR

O fleece that down her nape rolls, plume on plume!
O curls! O scent of nonchalance and ease!
What ecstasy! To populate this room
With memories it harbours in its gloom,
I'd shake it like a banner on the breeze.

Hot Africa and languid Asia play
(An absent world, defunct, and far away)
Within that scented forest, dark and dim.
As other souls on waves of music swim,
Mine on its perfume sails, as on the spray.

I'll journey there, where man and sap-filled tree
Swoon in hot light for hours. Be you my sea,
Strong tresses! Be the breakers and gales
That waft me. Your black river holds, for me,
A dream of masts and rowers, flames and sails.

A port, resounding there, my soul delivers
With long deep draughts of perfumes, scent, and clamour,
Where ships, that glide through gold and purple rivers,
Fling wide their vast arms to embrace the glamour
Of skies wherein the heat forever quivers.

I'll plunge my head in it, half-drunk with pleasure —
In this black ocean that engulfs her form.
My soul, caressed with wavelets there may measure
Infinite rockings in embalmèd leisure,
Creative idleness that fears no storm!

[110]

Blue tresses, like a shadow-stretching tent,
You shed the blue of heavens round and far.
Along its downy fringes as I went
I reeled half-drunken to confuse the scent
Of oil of coconuts, with musk and tar.

My hand forever in your mane so dense,
Rubies and pearls and sapphires there will sow,
That you to my desire be never slow—
Oasis of my dreams, and gourd from whence
Deep-draughted wines of memory will flow.

Translated by Roy Campbell

Cf: "A Hemisphere In Your Hair," page 31.

QUESTIONING AT MIDNIGHT

The clock, striking the midnight hour,
ironically summons us
to call to mind how we made use
of this *today* that's here no more:
—we have, today, prophetic day,
Friday the thirteenth!—in despite
of all we know that's good and right—
of heresy made great display;

yes, we've blasphemed the name of Jesus,
unquestionable God and Lord,
and, like a sycophant at the board
of some repulsive bloated Croesus,
to give the brute his filthy sport
we, Satan's loyal subject, have
affronted everything we love
and flattered what disgusts our heart;

and, cringing torturer, we've hurt
the weak, whom we scorned wrongfully,
but bowed low to Stupidity,
great bull-browed beast, throned and inert;
for it's brute Matter, dull as clay,
that these our pious lips have kissed,
and the pale radiance we've blessed
is but the corpse-light of decay;

and last, to drown our vertigo
in the full madness of despair,
we, haughty high-priest of the Lyre,
whose fitting glory is to show
the raptures of the works of death,
thirstless have drunk, and hungerless eaten!
Quick, quick! Blow out the lamp! Stay hidden
here in this gloom till our last breath.

Translated by Frederick Morgan

Cf: "One O'Clock In The Morning," page 15.

INVITATION TO THE VOYAGE

My child, my sister, dream
How sweet all things would seem
Were we in that kind land to live together,
    And there love slow and long,
    There love and die among
Those scenes that image you, that sumptuous weather.

    Drowned suns that glimmer there
    Through cloud-dishevelled air
Move me with such a mystery as appears
    Within those other skies
    Of your treacherous eyes
When I behold them shining through their tears.

There, there is nothing else but grace and measure,
Richness, quietness, and pleasure.

    Furniture that wears
    The lustre of the years
Softly would glow within our glowing chamber,
    Flowers of rarest bloom
    Proffering their perfume
Mixed with the vague fragrances of amber;
    Gold ceilings would there be,
    Mirrors deep as the sea,
The walls all in an Eastern splendor hung—
    Nothing but should address
    The soul's loneliness,
Speaking her sweet and secret native tongue.

There, there is nothing else but grace and measure,
Richness, quietness, and pleasure.

   See, sheltered from the swells
   There in the still canals
Those drowsy ships that dream of sailing forth;
   It is to satisfy
   Your least desire, they ply
Hither through all the waters of the earth.

   The sun at close of day
   Clothes the fields of hay,
Then the canals, at last the town entire
   In hyacinth and gold:
   Slowly the land is rolled
Sleepward under a sea of gentle fire.

There, there is nothing else but grace and measure,
Richness, quietness, and pleasure.

Translated by Richard Wilbur

Cf: "L'Invitation Au Voyage," page 32.

COMES THE CHARMING EVENING

Comes the charming evening, the criminal's friend,
Comes conspirator-like on soft wolf tread.
Like a large alcove the sky slowly closes,
And man approaches his bestial metamorphosis.

To arms that have laboured, evening is kind enough,
Easing the strain of sinews that have borne their rough
Share of the burden; it is evening that relents
To those whom an angry obsession daily haunts.
The solitary student now raises a burdened head
And the back that bent daylong sinks into its bed.
Meanwhile darkness dawns, filled with demon familiars
Who rouse, reluctant as business-men, to their affairs,
Their ponderous flight rattling the shutters and blinds.
Against the lamplight, whose shivering is the wind's,
Prostitution spreads its light and life in the streets:
Like an anthill opening its issues it penetrates
Mysteriously everywhere by its own occult route;
Like an enemy mining the foundations of a fort,
Or a worm in an apple, eating what all should eat,
It circulates securely in the city's clogged heart.
The heat and hiss of kitchens can be felt here and there,
The panting of heavy bands, the theatres' clamour.
Cheap hotels, the haunts of dubious solaces,
Are filling with tarts, and crooks, their sleek accomplices,
And thieves, who have never heard of restraint or remorse,
Return now to their work as a matter of course,
Forcing safes behind carefully re-locked doors,
To get a few days' living and put clothes on their whores.

[116]

Collect yourself, my soul, this is a serious moment,
Pay no further attention to the noise and movement.
This is the hour when the pains of the sick sharpen,
Night touches them like a torturer, pushes them to the open
Trapdoor over the gulf that is all too common.
Their groans overflow the hospital. More than one
Will not come back to taste the soup's familiar flavour
In the evening, with some friendly soul, by his own fire.

Indeed, many a one has never even known
The hearth's warm charm. Pity such a one.

Translated by David Paul

Cf: "Evening Twilight," page 44.

BEAUTY

I am as lovely as a dream in stone;
My breast on which each finds his death in turn
Inspires the poet with a love as lone
As everlasting clay, and as taciturn.

Swan-white of heart, a sphinx no mortal knows,
My throne is in the heaven's azure deep;
I hate all movement that disturbs my pose;
I smile not ever, neither do I weep.

Before my monumental attitudes,
Taken from the proudest plastic arts,
My poets pray in austere studious moods,

For I, to fold enchantment round their hearts,
Have pools of light where beauty flames and dies,
The placid mirrors of my luminous eyes.

Translated by F. P. Sturm

Cf: "Venus And The Motley Fools," page 10.